Bobby Owsinski's

GW00326500

Social Media Promotion
For Musicians

Second Edition

The Manual For Marketing Yourself,
Your Band, And Your Music Online

BOMG Publishing

Social Media Promotion For Musicians - Second Edition
The Manual For Marketing Yourself, Your Band, And Your Music Online
by Bobby Owsinski

Published by:
Bobby Owsinski Media Group
4109 West Burbank, Blvd.
Burbank, CA 91505

© Bobby Owsinski 2017
ISBN 13: 978-1-946837-95-0

To buy books in quantity for corporate use or incentives, call 818.588.6606 or email office@bobbyowsinski.com.

Introduction

Through the years, the capabilities of an artist or band has developed in a variety of areas far beyond just the music they create. Not only do we live in an age where the resources and technical power available to the musician for creating music is far greater than ever before, but he or she also has new abilities in developing an audience for that music as well. In fact, an artist, producer, engineer, manager, publisher, record label exec or any other creative person can now reach out directly to his fans, followers, customers or clients, and they're able to reach right back.

What this means is that it's now possible to communicate, promote, sell to and generally keep in touch with your audience without the need for a middleman like was needed in the past. In order to do that, you need to use the many online tools available to you, like the various social media networks (Facebook, Twitter, YouTube, Instagram and the like) coupled with a website, blog and email list among other things. The problem is that all these tools at our disposal can be virtually useless, not to mention time-consuming, without a strategy.

The whole premise of what I outline in *Social Media Promotion For Musicians*, and augment in the Music 3.0 blog, is the use of social media for promotion, not just personal use. Personal use is casual while promotional use is professional, and that makes a big difference when it comes to your online approach and mindset. You're not just reaching out to your family and friends, you're communicating with fans and clients (although some may also be your family and friends). There's a right way to do it, and there's a lot more that goes into it than meets the eye.

When it comes to using social media for promotion, the general idea is to keep the discourse professional (although it's okay to vary from that occasionally), provide your clients and fans with the latest information about your professional life, and measure how well that exchange of information takes place. The measurement part is at once the easiest and the toughest of the three. There's a lot of data available to you from all sorts of sources that you can't get from traditional media, but evaluating that info to see just how well you're doing isn't always easy.

Likewise, there's a timing issue to social media that's many times overlooked. It's not only important how you communicate, but when you do it as well. For every online communication method, there are certain times during the day and week that you'll most effectively reach the most people in and out of your network. This is one of the main issues in social media promotion and you'll find quite a bit about the latest studies in this book that can prove quite helpful to your online strategy.

Of course, the more information you have, the more efficient you become, which is important if you're a creative person of any type. One of the problems with social media is that it can be a runaway train of time and energy if you're not careful. Hopefully the information you find in this book will help you have more time to do the thing you do best and probably enjoy the most - create.

Social Media Promotion For Musicians looks at every area of your online life and shows you how to use it as a promotional tool. You'll learn the ins and outs of services and features that you didn't even know existed, and you'll learn exactly how to use them to your benefit, as well as the latest concepts in using social media for promotion.

So settle back and enjoy the book. You'll find a lot of information in this one place that you won't find anywhere else, and hopefully you'll find it most helpful to your career.

1

It's Called Promotion

There are a lot of books and articles that you can read that will provide some excellent information about using just about any social media service available online today. The trouble is, casually using a social network is not using it for promotion. Let's say that again:

Using Is Not Promotion

Promotion requires a much different set of tactics, which we'll cover in depth as we go along in the book. Not only are the methods different, but so is the mindset, since we're not talking about any kind of promotion, we're talking self-promotion, which can be singularly uncomfortable for many people.

The Meaning Of Self-Promotion

I grew up in a small town in rural Pennsylvania (population around 5,000) in a middle class family that believed in hard work as the means to get ahead in life. In my family (as well as many others in the area), you never unnecessarily talked about yourself with even the tinniest hint of self-satisfaction. If you were commended or received an award, it was expected that those outside the family would discover the fact through the natural buzz of people personally interacting, so there was no need to ever broadcast it yourself. To put it simply, self-promotion was the ultimate dirty word because it was somehow connected with an expanded ego.

Self-promotion doesn't have to be ego-induced bragging though, and that's exactly what I mean in the context of your online presence. It doesn't require you posting how great you are, trying to sell yourself, or an exhibition of any kind of elevated self-esteem. Most of us hate that kind of behavior online or offline anyway, and the results are mostly negative as a result.

No, self-promotion using social media is about three things: communicating, interacting, and measuring. It's more about telling your fans, friends and followers what you're doing and who you're working with, rather than how cool you are because of those facts. It's about letting your fans, clients and customers know you're still around before you're forgotten. It's about informing them that your new music is being released instead of trying to sell it to them. It's all about context. It's not about you as much as it is about the information about you. That's the first part of self-promotion.

The second part of self-promotion is about them - your friends, fans, followers, clients and customers. It's about you soliciting their opinions, answering their questions, listening to their views, and asking for their help. It's not about you, it's about *us*. We all move forward on this journey together. They move with you because there's something they really like about you or identify with (hopefully your music). You help keep the process moving by providing as much information as you can about your journey along the way.

The last part of self-promotion is measurement. This is something that could never be accomplished before in the detail it's done online today. Every measurement about your audience is increasingly granular, and that can either cause analysis paralysis or provide a better picture of just who all those fans and followers are. The measurement stats can show how many times a page on your site was visited, how long the viewer stayed, who viewed your post on any social network, how the person found it, where they live, and what computer operating system they use, among many other things. It can get scary how much we can learn about a fan or follower, or can be learned about us.

Although this sounds ominous, the bottom line is that the more we know about our fans and followers, the easier it is to give them what they want, nothing more or less. There are certain things they might love about you, but if you're unaware of what those thing are, you're likely posting the wrong content, which can lead to follower attrition. The measurement tools are easily available and they're mostly free, it's just up to you to use them in order to take advantage of their power.

Why Fan Data Matters

It's difficult to read a tech-related story these days without a reference to user data, metadata, or the latest popular term "Big Data" (large data sets controlled by mostly large companies), but there are a number of good reasons why this has become a major concern for artists, bands and businesses everywhere.

The biggest reason is that the more data you have about your fans and customers, the more you can take advantage of it for promotion as a result. That's because we're moving into a new era of marketing and promotion.

The future of marketing is micro-targeting.

The more you know about your fans, the easier it will be to send them only the information that they care about. Why inform a fan in St. Louis that you're doing a gig in Boston? There might be a time that you'd make that information available (if you're as big as Dave Matthews perhaps), but a few days before the show you just want to concentrate locally, and micro-targeting allows you to do that. What if you have a piece of merch that's aimed at your female fans in cold weather territories? Do you think the dudes care much about it? Do you think your female fans in Florida and Texas care much about it? Micro-targeting allows you to adjust your campaign accordingly.

And it makes measurement easier too. With a more precise user sample, it's much easier to tell if and how a campaign is actually working. If you shotgun a post to 3,000 fans and 15 respond, it looks like a response rate of only .5%, but if that same campaign was more precisely aimed at only 30 of those fans and you found that 12 responded, that's a whopping 40%. In the first example with a .5% response, you'd think that your campaign had a serious flaw in it. In the more targeted second example, we can see that the same campaign worked smashingly well. It all depends on targeting the right fans in the first place.

The old advertising days of "50% of advertising works. We just don't know which 50%," may soon be over, thanks to micro-targeting and better measurement techniques. It's all part of social self-promotion.

A Personal Story

Throughout this book I'll be giving you some personal experiences that I've had with social media promotion. The first I'd like to provide can be found below in Figure 1.1, which is a picture of me on ABC's 20/20 news show. Right after the second Obama inauguration in January 2013, I was asked to come on the show as their "music and recording expert" to provide a definitive answer to whether Beyonce lip-synced the "National Anthem."

Figure 1.1: Bobby Owsinski on ABC's 20/20

I received about three minutes of national media airtime in front of nearly two million people, but that's not the significant part of the story. No, the story really was how I was asked to do the show. It turns out that Chris Connelly, the show's host, is a fan of my daily music production blog. He found my blog through my posts on Twitter. When a story opportunity arose that he felt I could contribute to, he had his producer reach out to me to be on the show. The same thing happened when CNN asked me to share some thoughts as a branding expert regarding Justin Bieber "breaking his brand."

None of this would had ever happened if I didn't have a blog, nor would it have happened if I didn't frequently tweet about the blog posts. In other words, if it wasn't for social media, I never would've gotten the exposure on traditional media. It's one of the best examples of how social media promotion can work.

Social Media Promotion And The Music World

The reason why self-promotion can work in the music world today is because the basic structure of the music business has changed so much in the last decade. The Internet in all its forms has imposed many unexpected changes that many of the industry old guard consider a disaster, but everyone else considers a revolution. No longer are the record label gatekeepers needed as the business has truly changed in several ways.

The music business that we know today really started in a period that lasted from the 1950s until the early 1980s in the stage I call *Music 1.0* that has more or less remained in place for nearly 60 years (see Figure 1.2).

Figure 1.2: The business structure of Music 1.0

As you can see, the artist is signed to the label, who creates and manufactures the product, then sells it to the record store. In the meantime, the record label uses their own promotion department or independent promoters to persuade radio to play their releases, which the fan hears, and then might go to the record store to buy. In this case, the record label is the center of the music business world, and the artist is removed from any contact with that consumer and fan, except for maybe an official fan club.

The music business evolved to *Music 1.5,* which began in 1982 with the creation of the CD format. The CD quickly became a new high-profit revenue stream, thanks in part to the introduction of MTV, which soon turned into an unexpected new avenue for promotion. This led to ever-increasing sales that provided mountains of cash and profits, which brought a new-found respect from Wall Street, and before you knew it, four of the six major labels that were previously independently controlled were purchased by multi-national conglomerates. As a result of the new corporate ownership, an artist's image and the company's quarterly profits became more of a factor than the actual music, a trend that continues with large labels even today.

The day that the first MP3 digital music file was shared was the first day of *Music 2.0* (sometime around 1994). Although no one knew it at the time, this would soon become the disruption that would lead to the most major evolution in music business history, although at first it had little impact on overall sales. It wasn't long before record labels of all sizes became concerned about piracy, as record sales began to fall, and it became apparent the music industry needed to respond to the digital threat. Ironically, it was the computer industry that stepped in as its savior in 2001. While different digital-music services presented a wide range of alternatives to the labels to get paid for a download, Apple Computer's iTunes proved to be the business model that managed to actually monetize digital music and make it a true source of revenue. The revolution was now underway as the era of *Music 2.5* began.

The Current Music Business Structure

The music business truly changed forever in around 2010 with the inception of fifth generation of the music business called *Music 3.0*. It's a world where for the first time an artist could communicate, interact, market and sell directly to her audience, and they could communicate right back. This is something that true fans lusted for, with no bit of trivia too small, and it's what made Music 3.0 so powerful. Although we've progressed several stages beyond Music 3.0 business-wise, the same concept of artist-audience interaction is still in place.

The biggest change that came with Music 3.0 is in its structure, since the record label middlemen were now cut out of the loop (see Figure 1.3). The artist and the fan could now be directly in touch on any and every level they choose to be, from creation to promotion to marketing to sales. But merely staying in touch with a fan can be as fleeting as it sometimes is with friends or family. True fans, just like friends and family, want regular communication, and whether artists know it or not, so do they.

Figure 1.3: The business structure of Music 3.0

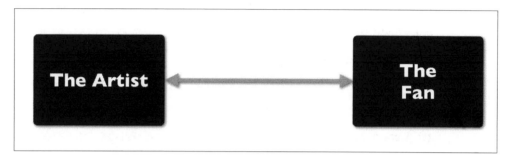

Music 3.0 allows the artist to promote and market directly to the fan. If you can reach the fan, you can make him aware of your products (music, gig tickets, and merchandise). If you can reach the fan, you can sell directly to her (although "offer a product" is a more accurate way of putting it). Most importantly, Music 3.0 allows you to have a dialog with the fan in order to help you understand how to better fine-tune the sales and marketing aspect of your business. What does the fan want? Just ask him. Does the fan want to be alerted when you come to town? Does the fan want a remixed version of a song? Would the fan be interested in a premium box set? By just asking, the fan will gladly let you know. And this is the essence of Music 3.0 - communication between the fan and the artist, or the ability of the artist to self-promote.

The New Audience

Another factor in Music 3.0 is that the audience has become niche oriented. From Brazilian marching band to Mandarin madrigal, if an artist searches long enough, he will find an audience. But although stratification of the audience means more opportunities for more artists, it also means that the possibility of a huge multi-million-selling breakout hit is diminished as fewer people are exposed to a single musical genre than ever before. Nearly gone are the days when a television appearance or heavy-rotation radio or MTV airplay can propel an artist to platinum-level success.

While remnants of the old Music 1.0 structure still exist (record labels, brick-mortar record stores, terrestrial radio, MTV, and so on) and can even be useful to the Music 3.0 artist, they will probably never again be the primary driving factor in the success of any artist. In a roundabout way, they never really were (the music is always the defining factor), although their influence was admittedly higher in the past.

It's said that a record label never signed an act because of its music; the label signed the act for the number of fans it either already had or had the potential of developing. If you had lines around the block waiting to see you play, the type or quality of the music really didn't matter that much to the label, because there was an audience that was willing to buy it. And so it is with Music 3.0, only now you can develop that audience in a more efficient way and actually make a living with a limited but rabid fan base.

As stated before, it's the first time where there can be no middleman if an artist choses not to have one. It's the first time that an artist can reach out directly to his fans, and they can reach back just as easily. It's an ecosystem that thrives on communication, and has a whole new set of rules for doing business as a result. It's an era finally adjusted for self-promotion - if you know how to do it.

Online Word Of Mouth

Social networks are now part of the fabric of our lives. Regardless of your age and where you live in the world, chances are that you've recently participated in a social network in some way. If we just look at the major social networks, we find that they have an enormous number of users as evidenced in Figure 1.4.

As you can see, both Facebook now has over two billion users and YouTube is over a billion, which means that if they were countries, either one could be the third largest in the world! MySpace is included as a reference, since at one time it was the most visited site on the Internet (yes, even more than Google for a bit) with more than 100 million active users at its peak.

Facebook is really the 800 pound gorilla in the social network world at the moment though, and the average user has around 155 Facebook friends. This piece of info is important since it's been estimated by Facebook itself that you can be connected to almost 2 billion people on the planet by only three and half people! Think of the promotional possibilities just within your near sphere of influence as a result!

That tiny bit of info goes to prove a point. *Social media is really online word-of-mouth.* This is important because it's been long established that word-of-mouth is the most effective form of advertising and promotion, and some new research from Nielsen backs the premise up yet again. In its most recent "Global Trust In Advertising Survey," the research company determined that:

- 83% of consumers trust word-of-mouth recommendations from friends and family above all else, compared to only 48% who trust online advertising.

- Online consumer reviews were the second most trusted form of advertising at 66%, which continues to hold steady year after year.

What this boils down to is that word of mouth always has been, and still is the most trusted form of promotion available, regardless of whether it's in-person or online. The only difference is that it's so much more powerful when done online.

Imagine having a face-to-face conversation with one of your friends and saying, "Dude, I am so happy with this new project that I've been working on with Dave Grohl. I put a lot of work into it, but it was worth it because I think it's coming out great." Somewhere down the road, that friend might then say to one of his friends, "I heard that John (you) was working on a pretty cool project with Dave Grohl and it's coming out great," who then tells another friend, who tells another friend. Before you know it, each friend has told anywhere from three to five friends (according to a study by Ford Motor Company done in 1986), depending upon how relevant and juicy the news was.

Now imagine posting the same news on Facebook, Twitter or any social network. You've now multiplied that reach by hundreds or thousands. Not only will your fans and followers repost your news online, but they'll probably physically tell their friends as well. This goes to show what a massive force-multiplier social media can be when it comes to promotion, especially when you consider the 155 average friends that each of your Facebook friends have.

The Theory of 22

While people may tell three to five friends about any good news, that same Ford study also found that something negative can spread even further. Ford found that a person with a complaint will tell an average of 22 people! Something that's merely displeasing may be communicated to only between five and ten.

This is why it's important that you learn to promote online the correct way, since any misstep can quickly get out of control and can potentially do more harm than good. This is one of the few cases where sometimes you're lucky if you're simply ignored.

That said, when it comes to marketing just about anything (including you and your music), social media should be a priority since it's an effective yet inexpensive platform for getting the word out that consumers deem credible.

8 Advantages Of Social Media Over Traditional Media

Social media holds quite of number of advantages over traditional media when it comes to promotion. It's the hub around which the online wheel that we live in today turns, and the following (inspired by marketing guru Simon Mainwaring) provides some of the reasons why.

1. Cost: Beyond your time and production costs, social media promotion is anywhere from free to very inexpensive. Traditional media has a high barrier to entry cost-wise.

2. Intimacy: Fans crave a personal interaction with the artist, band or brand and now it's possible. Traditional media broadcasts to thousands or millions of people at once, which is far less intimate.

3. Targeting: A large portion of the audience that traditional advertising reaches doesn't care about your message, which is a waste of money. Social media is able to target only those people that will respond to what you have to offer.

4. Nimbleness: Social media promotion allows you to respond to any changes in the market instantly, while traditional media requires a larger infrastructure that can't move as quickly.

5. Measurement: Social media has a variety of tools that can provide all sorts of data that's just not possible with traditional media.

6. Potential Growth: While a viral hit is unpredictable, just about any promotion has at least the chance of seeing exponential growth in a short period of time. Traditional media requires a significant investment to grow, and has nowhere near the possibilities provided by a post that's gone viral.

7. Participation: Social media allows artist to fan, and fan to fan, interaction to take place, while traditional media does not.

8. Proximity: Social media allows communication and interaction anywhere in the world. Traditional media is limited to the areas of the media buy.

We're lucky to live in a time where self-promotion is so inexpensive and easy. Once again, the biggest trick is knowing how to do it. Those tricks will be revealed as you read on.

Your Social Media Strategy

2

Most artists or bands use social media totally randomly. They create a Facebook page because that's what everyone does. They tweet because they heard Lady Gaga or Cold Play does that too. They create a Tumblr blog or join Instagram because they've been told it's the latest thing. The problem is that because there's no overall strategy for dealing with social media, it takes a lot of time to keep up with everything, and the more time you spend online, the less time you have for the fun things like creating.

But another problem with having no strategy is that social media becomes much less effective as a promotional tool as well. That's why this chapter looks at your overall online strategy, not just for social media. In the end, it's all tied together.

It's A Big Social Media World

By now everyone knows how powerful other social networks besides Facebook can be, but usually the only ones thought of are Twitter and, more recently, Instagram. There are a lot more than just those three though, and quite a few have very formidable numbers. According to MakeawebsiteHub, these are the networks that have at least 10 million monthly users.

1. Facebook - 1.59 B
2. WhatsApp - 1 B
3. QQ - 853 M
4. WeChat - 697 M
5. QZone - 640 M
6. Tumblr - 555 M
7. Instagram - 400 M
8. Twitter - 320 M
9. Google+ -300 M
10. Baidu Tieba - 300 M

11. Skype - 300 M
12. Viber - 249 M
13. Sina Weibo - 222 M
14. LINE - 215 M
15. SnapChat - 200 M
16. YY - 122 M
17. vKontakte (VK) - 100 M
18. Pinterest - 100 M
19. LinkedIn - 100 M
20. Telegram - 100 M

21. Reddit - 100 M
22. Taringa - 75 M
23. Foursquare - 40 M
24. Renren - 30 M
25. Tagged - 25 M

26. Badoo - 20 M
27. MySpace - 20 M
28. StumbleUpon - 10 M

As you can see, there are plenty that you probably don't recognize, mostly because they're popular in an area of the world other than North America, but that doesn't mean they're any less powerful in getting your message across.

TIP: When determining your social strategy, ask your customers which network they visit most often, and be prepared to concentrate your efforts there.

The Problems And The Solutions

It's probably no surprise that four out of five Internet users regularly visit social networks and blogs, and as you're probably well aware, it takes a fair amount of time to participate in only the largest ones, let alone any of the other alternatives. In fact, the average person:

- posts 90 pieces of Facebook content per month

- spends 23 minutes a day on Twitter

- watches 124 videos equaling 3.75 hours of video on YouTube a month

That's plenty of time right there that probably isn't as productive as you'd like it to be. The last chapter discussed how just using a social network wasn't enough; you have to know how to use it for promotion. Now you can see that there's an additional problem, this one regarding time. It's possible to spend so much time maintaining your social media accounts that you never have time for anything else.

The solution, of course, is to have a total online strategy, and there are three reasons why this is important:

- **Efficiency**: so you spend less time online for the same results or better.

- **Effectiveness**: your fan base increases and you're better at giving them what they want.

- **Message Control**: you have total control of your brand and how it's presented

Attaining any one of these items makes it worth the effort to develop a strategy, but put all three together and it becomes a no-brainer. The problem is that there are so many online social sites and services, not to mention your main website, blog, music and video hosting site, that it's easy to get confused or sidetracked by the sheer breadth of it all. Luckily, there's help.

The Big Picture

There are a lot of online elements that every artist, band or brand has to be involved in these days in order to be an effective online marketer. It's pretty easy to get confused and either not know where to begin, or throw yourself scattershot at all of them, which usually means that your efforts will be ineffective when it comes to promotion. If we just look at the major components, it looks something like this:

- Your website   - Music releases

- Your email list   - YouTube video posts

- Facebook posts   - Blog posts

- Twitter or Instagram posts

Throw in any of the 100+ additional networks available and it's no wonder why artists, bands and music execs become bewildered by it all. We can make things a bit simpler by separating these components so they fall into one of three categories; content, interaction and tactics. If we break all this out, it looks like this:

Content: The places online where you place the material that you generate, like information about your band, music, videos, or blog posts. Interaction in all the social networks where you might interact with your fans and followers. These include:

- Your website

- Your mailing list

- Your blog

- Your videos on Youtube, Facebook, and other video sites

- Your music files on Soundcloud or other music hosting sites

Interaction: The places where you regularly communicate with your fans, followers, clients and customers. These include:

- Facebook

- Twitter

- Instagram

- Google+

- Pinterest

- Any other social network

Tactics: Everything required to define and refine who you are and your position in the online world. These include:

- Branding

- Strategy

- Measurement

All this gets more interesting when we put into the form of a Venn chart as in Figure 2.1 and watch how the categories intersect.

Figure 2.1: A Venn chart of your online presence.

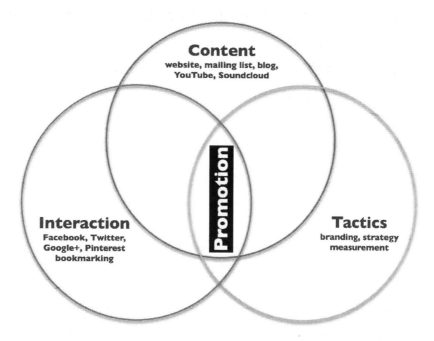

As you can see, where all three category circles cross, a new element pops up - *promotion*. This isn't possible without all three elements combined, which goes to show just how synergistic they all are. Use only one or two and you fall short; use all three and new possibilities for promotion arise. That's not the strategy though, only the general overview.

Developing Your Online Strategy

The biggest difficulty artists, bands, musicians, producers, songwriters, publishers and even record labels have when it comes to social media is that they don't have an online focus. They may have a website, but rely on Facebook for most of their traffic. Maybe it's a Tumblr or Wordpress blog that gets the most attention, with a Facebook page getting some consideration depending on the whim of the day. Even worse, maybe they have a website, Facebook page, blog, Twitter account, mailing list, Instagram account and more, and all get random attention. The problem is, until you have a single focal point online, you don't really have a strategy. That's where your website comes in as your primary online element.

Don't Depend On An External Site

Unfortunately, a website many times gets overlooked as an integral piece of your digital promotional life because there are so many other places that you can use as your online focal point. Having a Facebook page or Tumblr blog, or relying on another social network as your online central focus has a number of potential flaws, not the least is control of your message. Let's look at three scenarios where relying on a social media site as your main contact point can prove disastrous.

- **Scenario #1:** Our first scenario is a real-life example of a band I'll hypothetically call "The Unknowns," since one of the band members asked me not to reveal their true name. During the heyday of MySpace around 2004 the band was hot and eventually developed a following of over 900,000. This led to a number of record labels becoming interested (remember that they sign you for your audience, not your music), with the band eventually signing a big deal with one of the largest major labels at the time. The label immediately told the band to suspend their MySpace account because "we can do all that better in-house than you can." In typical record company fashion, the label ultimately did very little for the band's online presence. They did create a new slicker label-managed MySpace account, but they were not able to transfer any of the band's previous followers, thus leaving them with a presence that was far less than they had before they were signed. Of course, when The Unknown's album was released they had no way to alert those 900,000 followers since they didn't have any of their email addresses, and they didn't even have a website where their fans could go in order to discover the latest news about them. Needless to say, the album bombed and the band was dropped from the label. They never recovered that massive fan base that they had before they were signed.

The moral of the story is that if they had redirected those fans from their MySpace account to their website in order to harvest at least some of the email addresses, things might've turned out a lot differently, since they could have alerted their fans when the album was released. And that's the problem with relying on an external social media site that you don't control as your focal point online.

It's too easy for today's artist who only dabbles in social networking to get complacent and comfortable with the abilities of a single social network, but that can spell disaster for maintaining your fan base if you're not careful. As those artists who formerly depended upon MySpace now know, what's hot today can be ice cold tomorrow. But other negative scenarios also exist that can be far worse than the network falling out of favor.

This scenario was recently played out again in early 2013 in a slightly different manner when MySpace relaunched an updated version of its site. Every single artist lost all of their followers, and every MySpace user lost their previous settings, and any affiliation with the artists they were following. All users had to reregister again, and all artists, regardless of how popular they were (even co-owner Justin Timberlake), started all over again with zero followers!

- **Scenario #2:** Let's say that you've cultivated a huge following on Facebook. What would happen if Facebook was purchased by EXXON (impossible, but let's pretend), who decides that all it wants is the underlying technology of the network, and shuts the rest down? If you didn't capture the contact info of all your followers, you'd lose them to the nothingness of cyberspace. Don't laugh - a scenario like this could happen, but most likely on another smaller network.

- **Scenario #3:** What would happen if Facebook (I'm picking on them because they're the big dog on the social block) changes its terms of service, and now charges you $0.25 for every fan past 100? If you're lucky enough to have 8,000 fans, it's going to cost you $2,000 to continue. Or what if they decided to limit everyone's fan connections to 100? Both are unlikely, but something similar has already happened, where suddenly you're unable to access that large fan base that you've worked so hard to develop unless you pay for the privilege (I'll explain more later in the book).

The point of all of the above scenarios is that when you depend on a social network for your online presence, you're ceding control to an unknown, unseen force that can change its will at any time with no regard to your online well-being. That's why it's imperative that you don't count on a single social network for your total online presence or even your social media presence. If you rely on an external network, sooner or later you're going to get burnt. It's the nature of the Internet to constantly change, and it's too early to get a feel for the life span of even of the largest sites and networks.

Just to illustrate the volatile nature of social networks, in 2005 MySpace was the most visited social network online with 100 million users. A mere five years later and it had dropped below 25 million, yet has doubled that number and is slowly growing again but it's hardly considered a must-be-on network. What this means is that you must pick and choose the social networks that you participate in wisely, and always engage in a number of networks in case one suddenly falls out of favor.

Relying On Too Many Sites

Another common mistake that artists sometimes make is having too many contact points (like their website, blog, Facebook, Tumblr and ReverbNation, for example) all requiring separate updates. You can imagine how tough it is to keep every one of those sites updated regularly. Worse is the fact that it's confusing for the fan, who just wants a single place to visit. When you don't have a plan, it takes a lot of time to maintain your accounts and the updates and posts happen randomly or not at all, which can lead to follower attrition. Yet another problem is that you may be collecting email addresses from each site and they may all be going on different mailing lists.

The quick solution is to use one site (usually your website) as a your main focal point and use that to feed daily updates and info to all the others via RSS or social-media broadcast tools like Tweetdeck or Hootsuite.com (which we'll cover later in the book). This means that you only need to update a single site and all the others will be updated at the same time, although it's good practice to customize the post for each slightly.

The Center Of Your Online Universe

The second component of this management strategy would be to have all of your satellite sites (blog, Facebook, and so on) designed in such a way as to feed your social media viewers into your website (see Figure 2.2). At a bare minimum, the email registration of each satellite site should feed into the same list service provider as your main site.

Figure 2.2: The center of your online universe

That's not to say that you don't want to communicate with fans or clients on Facebook, Twitter or your blog. It just means that whenever it's appropriate, you link them back to your site. You do this so they're always aware that the main information about you (like tour dates, video and song releases, contact and booking information, etc.) can be found there, and you can capture their email address for your mailing list so you can communicate directly to them without the randomness of a social network.

As you'll see in Chapter 4, there's a host of additional reasons why having a strong website is important, even if it's not updated often. You may use other parts of your online presence more, but few are as effective for doing business.

The Steps To A Successful Online Strategy

Although you'll find plenty of detailed information in this book about most aspects of your online strategy, here are the six basic steps you'll need to take in order to prepare for online promotion.

1. **Make your website your main online focal point.** Make sure that all your important information is curated there and is easy for a site visitor to find. Chapter 4 will describe what a modern artist website needs to look like and how it should function.

2. **Create accounts on the "Big 4" social networks** (Facebook, Twitter, Instagram and YouTube). You can't be everywhere at once. Even if you could it would take so much time that you'd never have any time to make music, which is what we're trying to avoid. That said, in order to get the most out of social media promotion, you need the following:

   - **A Facebook page.** Regardless of how you feel about Facebook, you still need a presence on it if for no other reason than it's easy proximity to lots of potential new fans. If you're just starting out, you might want to start with a personal page instead of a fan site though. It can be embarrassing to have a fan page with only a few followers, and a personal site is a way to gain some momentum before you make the leap. We'll cover the ins and outs of Facebook in Chapter 6.

   - **A Twitter account.** The people that dismiss Twitter are the ones that aren't aware of how to use it for promotion. It's extremely powerful for attracting new fans and keeping your current ones instantly informed. We'll look at Twitter in Chapter 7.

   - **A YouTube channel.** Videos are such a major part of any musician, artist or band's online presence that you really need your own channel to exploit them successfully. Chapter 9 will describe how.

   - **An Instagram account.** Instagram is not yet an absolutely necessary network to participate in, but it's still growing and has a number of unique features that work particularly well for anyone in the music business. We'll delve into Instagram more in Chapter 8.

- **A look at other networks.** As I've pointed out previously, there are a ton of other social networks and a many of them might deserve your attention at some point. There comes a point where the amount of time invested versus the potential outcome just doesn't balance out, which is why you should probably stay with the previous four networks, or even just a few of them, until you're really comfortable before you decide take on another one. The only exception to that would be if a big portion of your audience is on a particular network other than the "Big 4," then you might want to substitute that network for Instagram.

3. Use a social media broadcast app for all your updates. An app like Tweetdeck or Hootsuite is one of the keys to streamlining the process that saves time and makes what you do online more efficient. We'll discuss these and other similar apps throughout the book.

4. Develop your social media sites so they all feed viewers into your main site. The key is to make sure that any viewer on any site is aware that you have a website and knows that it's the main repository of information about you.

5. Be sure that email list subscribers from all sites go to same master list provider. Different mailing lists don't do you much good if you have to create a separate newsletter blast for each one. We'll look at mailing lists, list providers, and newsletters in Chapter 5.

6. Get third party help when you get to the point where you're overwhelmed. If your popularity as an artist is growing, at some point social-media management gets too complex to maintain and third-party help is needed. This is usually a good thing, since that means you've progressed to where things are so massive that you can't keep up. Furthermore, a company that specializes in social-media management can keep you current with new tools and techniques that you might not be aware of. Even when outside help arrives, remember that you're still the one that drives the bus. Be sure to take part in all strategy discussions, but leave the actual facilitation to the company or person that you've hired.

Having a sound social strategy is the key to successful promotion. The upcoming chapters of this book will examine each of the above points in much more detail as you learn the ins and outs of how this is accomplished.

TIP: The order of importance of your online components is (1) website, (2) mailing list, (3) Facebook, (4) YouTube, (5) Twitter or Instagram, (6) blog. The order of importance of numbers 3 to 6 may change, but your website and mailing list will always be the most important.

3

Developing Your Brand

Before you begin any promotion you have to know exactly what it is that you're promoting. In this case, the product is you, your music, and your image. Put them together and they become your "brand."

Whenever the word "brand" is spoken to musicians their eyes usually glaze over faster than an air guitar contest, and understandably so. Branding smacks of marketing, which is business, not art. Every musician wants to stay in their comfort zone, which is creating art, and that's the reason why they entered into the music business in the first place.

But it's called the music "business" for a reason. If you're playing music (or producing, engineering, publishing, songwriting, etc.) for any reason more than a hobby, commerce enters into the equation, and the more in-demand you are, the more money you'll make. Whether you know it or not, you are a brand. The problem is that most of us aren't aware of what our brand, or any brand for that matter, really is.

What Is A Brand?

One of the things that an artist or band hears a lot these days is the need to promote "your brand" in order to get ahead in the current era of the music business. That's all well and good, but you can't promote your brand unless you know the definition of a brand in the first place. So what exactly is a brand?

A brand is a promise of quality and consistency.

Want a few good examples of a brand in everyday life? How about MacDonald's for starters. No matter where in the world you go, you can always recognize a McDonald's franchise by the now-famous golden arches, and you know that a Big Mac will taste like a Big Mac. Beijing, Cleveland, Amsterdam, Sydney, Johannesburg, or Sao Paulo - it will always taste the same.

Then there's Coke. First you have the distinctive script logo and the signature shaped bottle, then you have the exact same taste from bottle to can to fountain (unless they get the syrup to carbonated water mixture slightly wrong). Once again, anywhere in the world, a Coke's a Coke. When Coke tried to change the formula in 1985, they unwittingly broke their brand and had to fight to get their customers back because the trust in the brand was damaged.

If we look to the world of electronics, there's Apple. First you have the identifying one-bite-of-the-apple logo that's so strong that you don't even need to have the name spelled out. Then no matter what product you purchase from Apple, you can expect a sleek high-tech design and an easy to understand user interface.

If we look to the world of music, there's Fender, which was the world's leading brand for guitars and guitar amplifiers until CBS bought them in 1965. Slowly but surely, the new owners broke the brand because they neither understood the market nor cared about the quality of the product. The once mighty Fender name became an insignia for ill-conceived products that didn't work nearly as well as they once did. It was only when management purchased the company from CBS in 1985 that Fender was able to gradually restore it's brand to where it is today as once again one of the great names in musical instruments, but it took more than ten long years to recover.

Artist Branding

For an artist, a brand means a consistency of persona, and usually a consistency of sound. Regardless of what genre of music the artist delves into, the feel is the same and you can tell it's none other than that artist. Madonna has changed musical and fashion directions many times during her career but her brand remained consistent. Her post-feminist persona remained the same even as she changed to and from the "Material Girl." The Beatles experimented with a wide variety of directions, but you never once questioned who you were listening to. It was always fresh and exciting, yet distinctly them. The same goes for any of the legacy acts that have lasted 20+ years, which is why they lasted that long.

On the other hand, Neil Young almost killed his career with an electronic album called *Trans* that alienated all but his hardiest fans, and the well-respected voice of Sound Garden, Chris Cornell, did irreparable harm to his solo career thanks to his loop-based electronic pop album with Timbaland (*Scream*). Why did this happen? For both artists, the album no longer "felt" like them. Both Young and Cornell built their careers on organic music played with a band, and as soon as their music became regimented and mechanical, the consistency (and some say the quality) of their brands was lost. After *Trans*, Young returned to his roots and slowly built his brand back to superstar level over time, and Cornell eventually went back to sing with Sound Garden, which rebuilt his rock credibility.

How do you determine what your brand is? It's easier said than done. In order for an artist to successfully promote their brand, they must have a great sense of self-awareness. You must know who you are, where you came from, and where you're going in terms of your music and your career. You must know what you like and don't like, and what you stand for and why. And you must have an inherent feel for your sound and what works for you, which is usually against the grain of a current trend unless you happen to be leading it.

TIP: Brand self-awareness sometimes differentiates a superstar from a star, and a star from someone who wants it really badly but never seems to get that big break.

The Three Pillars Of A Successful Brand

One of the problems with the process of branding is that by being such an obvious goal, it can feel like a sell-out. That very well may be true in some cases were the branding is created more to manipulate an artist to fit into a trend rather than as a promotional strategy to build the artist's audience.

The problem is that whether you like it or not, if you're an artist, you're already a brand. It may not be a strong brand, but then again, it very well may be stronger than you think without any thought or effort on your part. What I want to outline here are the elements that make up a brand and how they're created.

So what are the pillars of building the brand? There are three:

- **Familiarity**: You can't have a brand unless your followers or potential followers are familiar enough with who you are. They don't even have to know what you sound like to be interested in you if you have a buzz and they've heard about you enough to want to check you out. Amanda Palmer, who more people know for her social media savvy than her music, fits into this category. Or you can like the Red Bull brand without drinking Red Bull.

- **Likeability**: Your followers have to like you or something about you. It could be your music, or it could be your attitude or your image. You could even say how much you hate your fans and do everything to ridicule them, and that irreverent manner could be just the thing they like about you. It doesn't matter what it is, but there has to be something they like. Most artists fall into this category.

- **Similarity**: Your fans have to feel that either you represent them in a cause or movement (like a new genre of music), or that someday they can be you. Female Olympic athletes usually don't do well in this category because their sleek and muscular look is so far beyond what the ordinary girl or women can attain that they can't relate to them. On the other hand, young girls used to love Taylor Swift because they felt that she could be their best friend from next door.

If you have those three things along with a product that consistently maintains its quality (your music), you've got a brand. I wouldn't intentionally try to manufacture your brand so it absolutely complies with these pillars (people usually see right through that), but always keep in mind that this is how your audience views you, although none of them may even realize it.

8 Steps To Discovering Your Brand

Your brand is the experience fans or clients have when doing business or engaging with you. This can be either intentional or accidental. You're either actively creating it, or you leave it up to others to make of you what they will.

Ask yourself the following 8 questions to help discover your brand:

1. What name do I use? Do I use the name that's most comfortable to me now? Do I use the name I prefer to be called by now?

2. What makes me stand out from everyone else? What do I do? How would I like to be perceived? List your core specialties, then narrow it down to 3, then narrow it to 1.

3. Who do I wish to serve? How do I do it? Describe your audience. Describe the people you would like to be your audience, or the ones you'd like to attract.

4. What is my image? How do others describe me? Ask a variety of people, then extract the commonalities.

5. What's my personality like? How do people feel when they work with me?

6. What do I stand for? Is there a cause I really believe in? What are my values? What really matters to me? What would I never do?

7. What's my look? What colors do I like? What type of clothes do I wear? Do I look better in certain colors? Does my name suggest an image?

8. Is there a current brand that I identify with? Why?

It's quite common to not be able to answer many of these at one sitting. They take some time and thought, so be prepared to do some research to discover the answers that accurately portrays your brand. There are a few things that you can do right now though:

- Pick a consistent name, and also a sub-title that describes your image

- Pick a color

- Pick a font

These three things will give you a head start on your branding in that they'll provide a consistency across all your promotional material, packaging, and online presence.

Developing Your Brand

While the music that you play or create is totally up to you and outside the realm of this book, what we can deal with is the second part of the brand - your image. Here are some steps to take to refine your brand.

1. Make sure your brand image accurately portrays your music and personality. If you're a biker band, you probably don't want a website that's all pink and flowery. On the other hand, the pink works great for Katy Perry. Likewise, if you're an EDM artist you wouldn't want your site to show the woods and trees, although that could work well for an alt rock band from Minnesota or someone doing music for meditation.

2. Keep it honest and simple. Don't try to be who you're not, it's too hard to pull off. You are who you are and people will either love you for it or they won't. While you can concoct a backstory where you were taught a new form of music by aliens, then honed your technique in the jungles of Brazil, that just sets your brand up to fail if you really can't live up to the image that's been painted. Best to keep things simple and be honest about who and what you are and where you came from. If people like what you do and can relate to you, that will shine through and your fans will not only find it interesting enough, but will be totally fascinated as well.

3. Differentiate yourself. While it might seem tempting to proclaim that you're just like Coldplay, that doesn't immediately make you their equal in the eyes of the public. The fact of the matter is, there already is a Coldplay, why does the world need another one? It's their brand, not yours. The only way that a brand can be successful is to differentiate itself from the competition. A great example is the seminal punk band The Ramones, who decided that all their songs would be as short as possible and played without solos. There must be something that makes you unique in even a small way. If you can't find it, it may be time to go back to the drawing board.

4. Keep the look consistent. Consistency of product and image are the key to branding. That's why you need to use the same logo and fonts and have the same general look and feel across all your promo for it to be effective. That includes your website, press kit, blog, newsletter and all social media.

5. Create a remarkable logo. This is a requirement if you're planning to promote your brand. You need this for your website, social sites, merchandise, press kit, promo and on your stage during gigs. In short, it has to be part of everything you do. You may start promoting yourself without it, but it's a big plus if you already have a logo. It separates you from the newbies. Just as an example, here are a few unmistakable musician's logos in Figure 3.1.

If you're a musician without a band, a producer, songwriter or engineer, it doesn't mean that you must also have a logo as well (although it would help), but at the very least, use the same font for your name on your blog, website, newsletter and anywhere else it might appear.

Figure 3.1: Recognizable Band Logos

6. Great photos are a necessity. You need first class photos for posters, merch, website, social networks, press kits, and a lot more if you want to build your brand. This is as important as the logo - you need a great photo in order to begin any kind of promotion. Have you ever seen a Facebook page or website of a major artist without an artist or band photo?

7. Give away samples. Learn this phrase well as it will be repeated throughout this book.

Your music is your marketing.

That means that you can't look at your music as your product. It may bring in some money eventually but not all that much in the grand scheme of things. Remember that 90 to 95% of the money that a major artist earns is *not* from recorded music. It's from concerts, merchandise, publishing and licensing.

TIP: Don't be afraid to give your music away. It's your best marketing tool and the best way to build your brand.

---

8. Cool is never declared. You cannot proclaim how new and unique you are. If such a statement is in fact true, people will find out soon enough and tell the world. You can use quotes from other people, but telling the world that you think you're cool does not make it so.

These are not the only steps that you can take, but they'll take you a long way to creating a brand image that works for you.

Why A Trademark Can Be Important

If you've established your logo or a unique look to your brand, it can be quite beneficial to have it trademarked. The reason is that not only can it provide an additional income stream at some point, but it can also provide some protection as well. First, let's look at exactly what a trademark is.

A Trademark is any unique symbol, design, mark or words that distinguishes your product from others in the marketplace.

An example of a trademark could be the Nike swoosh, the design of the Coke bottle, or the McDonald's golden arches. These are all trademarks because you identify the design with their product without ever considering a similar product. The mark separates the brand from the competition around it.

Here's why having a trademark can be important. Let's say your band name is "Shooting Star" and you're based in Birmingham, Alabama. You begin to play a club circuit that leads you from Florida to Nashville and you're becoming pretty popular. If you've not trademarked the name "Shooting Star," there's nothing to prevent another band from taking the same name and calling up that club in Tallahassee you just played at a few weeks ago and booking a gig using the same name without telling the club they're a different Shooting Star. You may have used the name first, but unless it's trademarked, you have no legal recourse.

Another reason owning your trademark can be important is when you're signed to a record label. If at some point you have a falling out, there's no reason why the label can't put out an album of your outtakes to try to make some money without your knowledge (it's been done plenty of times before). If you owned your trademark however, they'd be legally forced to come to you to license the logo (the trademark) before they could either sell or promote the album.

Yet another reason is merch. If you've become popular enough that merch emblazoned with your name has some value to it, there's nothing to stop a street vendor from running off a hundred T-shirts and selling them outside your gig before your fans even get inside the door to look at your official merch. They may still do it if you own your trademark, but at least you would have a legal recourse to have them cease and desist from selling them. If you don't own your trademark, you may be out of luck.

Acquiring A Mark

There are two ways to acquire a trademark; the cheap and easy way, and the expensive way. As with most things in life, you get what you pay for.

The easy way is to just start use the ™ trademark symbol on your branding. This is called a "common law" trademark, and all that's required is that you just begin using it before anyone else, as in the case of the band name. The problems with this are that you must continually use the mark without any breaks or the mark offers you little protection. Your protection also can be fairly limited even with a continuos mark and may even be restricted to a certain location. Plus, you're not able to register for an international trademark.

The second way requires an official registration with the US Patent and Trademark Office (uspto.gov) and is indicated with an R in a circle like this - ®. It costs anywhere from $275 to $325, but is complicated enough that you probably want an attorney to submit the registration for you in order to ensure that you're properly protected. The value of a registered trademark is that it's the ultimate protection for your mark, and it then allows you to apply for a trademark in other countries as well.

Trademarks can be a complex area of the law where you definitely should have advice from an attorney, but it will give you the optimum protection and control that could turn into an income stream somewhere down the road.

I'm With The Brand

It seems that as music stars becomes more popular, so too does their desire to cash in on their fame through what's known as "brand extension." That used to be quite contrary to what many artists were originally about, preferring to not lend their image to anything not directly involved in their music, but today it's just a matter of fact. Just as an example, here's how a number of high-profile artists have extended their brands with products that aren't exactly tied to music.

- Aerosmith guitarist Joe Perry has his own line of hot sauce.

- The r&b singer Usher teamed up with Mastercard to launch a range of credit cards.

- Brit pop legend Cliff Richards, Boz Scaggs, Mick Hucknall (Simply Red), Dave Matthews, Mick Fleetwood, Les Claypool, Jonathan Cain (Journey), Maynard James Keenan (Tool, Perfect Circle), AC/DC, Olivia Newton John, David Coverdale (Whitesnake) and L'il Jon all produce their own wines.

- Justin Bieber has, curiously for a guy, his own line of nail polish called *One Less Lonely Girl*.

- Madonna opened the *Hard Candy Fitness* centre in Mexico City, the first of what she hopes will be a worldwide chain of gyms.

- Lady Gaga has released her own range of Heartbeat headphones.

- Beyoncé is now focusing on her clothing lines, *House of Dereon* and *I Am Sasha Fierce*.

- Jay-Z has non-musical business opportunities including the clothing label Rocawear, the New York nightclub 40/40, and a sports agency.

- 50 Cent, Eminem and Sean Combs (P. Diddy) all have their own clothing ranges, while Combs has also carved out an extra source of income for himself in promoting the vodka brand *Cîroc*.

- Katy Perry, Hillary Duff, Avril Lavigne, Mariah Carey, Britney Spears, Justin Bieber, Fergi, and host of other music celebs have their own fragrance lines.

This may or may not be the right way to go depending upon how you feel about commercialism in music, but some artists want to take advantage of every opportunity that their brand might bring, and consumer products are a way to go.

Brands And Social Media

Assuming that you maintain your brand integrity, here are few interesting facts from Atym Marketing Research about how social media plays into building that brand.

- 29% of Twitter users follow a brand.

- 39% have tweeted about a brand.

- 29% have retweeted about a brand.

- 58% of Facebook users have liked a brand.

- 42% have mentioned a brand in a status update.

- 41% have shared a link, video or story about a brand.

- 66% of people who have liked a brand have 100 or more Facebook friends.

The point of the stats above is that people who like brands are very active on social media and greatly influence others. That alone should be a good enough reason why social media should always be a main part of your brand building and overall marketing strategy.

Creating Your Killer Website

4

If you've read the previous chapters, you know how important a website can be to your branding and online strategy. That's said, just having a website that's not particularly well-conceived or designed can be only a few steps better than having none at all. It still takes the right elements and implementation to make a site effective.

The Elements Of A Successful Site

A website should be unique and individual when it comes to its design, and that means it should obviously reflect your brand and your music. That said, if we were to look at the ideal website we would find the following common elements:

The Site Name

The name of the site has to be easy to spell and remember, and it's best if it has a ".com" behind it rather than ".net," ".us," or other type of extension, although that's not absolutely necessary these days. Let's say that your band is called "The Unsigned." That means that the strongest URL would be "theunsigned.com." If that URL is not available, try some simple alternates like "theunsignedband.com," "unsignedband.com," or "unsignedtheband.com"

What you don't want is something that's so clever that people can't remember it, like "theun$igned.com." No matter how brilliant you think this is, you're going to have people confused on how to pronounce it, and you can't be sure that they'll actually type the $ sign into the search engine correctly when searching for your site.

Yet another problem is making it so long that it's unmemorable, like "theunsignedbandfrommaryland.com." You probably won't have much trouble registering the URL, but it won't matter because it's so long that it's difficult to read and way too difficult for someone to type correctly because it has so many characters.

The next problem is to make sure that the website URL doesn't present an unintentional double entendre. There are some classic bad ones that illustrate the point, like the website that displays the names of the agents that represent a certain celebrity called *Who Represents*. The URL is a different story as it reads "whorepresents.com." Then there's the site *Therapist Finder* who's URL reads "therapistfinder.com." Or the *Italian Power Generator* company who's URL reads "powergeneratorlia.com." Or the art designers with their "speedofart.com." Make sure you take a step back and read that URL before you commit to it so you won't be embarrassed later.

The Visual Design

The look of your site has to reflect your brand, as was discussed in Chapter 3. What that means is that there's no sense making it dark and menacing if you're a pop band, or making it flowery and colorful looking if you're an EDM artist. That said, here are a number of basic points to consider with your design.

1. Use the screen real estate wisely.

- Keep the most important content "above the fold," or at the top of the screen where the reader doesn't have to scroll down.

- Watch out for clutter. Achieve a balanced layout by designing no more than three focal points by using the "big, medium, small" strategy.

- Provide enough white space around elements so that they're visually distinguishable, but don't leave big areas of blank screen.

2. Specify fonts that are designed for the screen.

- Sans-serif fonts (those without the little tails on some of the characters) generally works the best (Verdana, Tahoma, Arial), although some serif fonts work okay (Georgia). Stay away from Times as it's designed for newspapers and can feel dated. Use any decorative font you want in a logo image, but stay away from browser decorative fonts (**Impact**, *Comic Sans*) that draw more attention than the copy itself.

- Only use two font families per page or site *at most*, and then only to contrast headings to text, or sidebar to main content.

- Format paragraphs and other content for the best readability

  - **Use *text-align: left*** for blocks of text.

  - **Use *text-align: center*** occasionally for a page heading or a special effect. but never for text blocks.

  - **Use *text-align: right*** to connect form labels with their data entry boxes or to connect left-hand captions to their associated images.

  - **Use *text-align: justify*** only if the column is wide enough so that it doesn't leave blocks of white space down the middle.

3. Avoid using fonts smaller than 10 point (depending on the font).
One of the things that site visitors hate the most is having to zoom in to read something.

4. Fit the color scheme to the purpose of the site.

- A good bet is to select your colors based on your logo or an important image on the page.

- Like fonts, use one main color and one secondary color for a page or site; a third color might provide emphasis or contrast.

- Check for sufficient contrast between text and background, and also check that the contrast works for any color-blind visitors.

- Never use color alone to provide information.

5. Design For Mobile

Be sure that your site is built to display on a mobile browser. Don't forget that the world we now live in is a mobile one, and it's going to be even more so in the future. Make sure that your site looks good on a phone or tablet before confirming it as complete.

- Check the layout to be sure that everything shows up where you expect it on the screen.

- Check the readability of the text to be sure that the information on the site is useful to the visitor.

The Navigation

Many artist websites are quickly designed without much thought, and that makes the user experience somewhat less than elegant. Before you begin to design or redesign your site, consider these six tips to improve its navigation.

1. Keep it consistent. Consistent navigation from page to page in both how and where things appear on the site promotes ease of use and increases your visitor's ability to find relevant information more quickly.

2. Divide categories clearly. All categories must be clearly and visually defined, with category headings separated visually from sub-categories.

3. Keep the menu hierarchy to three. It's best to keep it to main idea, topic, and subtopic.

4. Make all navigation elements clickable links. All major category headings should be clickable links, even though you may have a drop-down menu with sub-categories.

5. Use accurate navigation titles. Visitors need a general idea of what they should find on a page even before they click on a navigation link.

6. Always test your site. Make sure that every link functions correctly before it goes live. This not only ensures a better user experience, but a better search ranking as well.

These are very simple points that will lead to a much better user experience, which is not only what we all want from a website, but one of the things that Google bases its search ranking on.

The Content

The content of your page is important in a number of ways. First, it's all the information that you want your site visitors to know, but it's also important from an SEO standpoint (Search Engine Optimization). Here are a couple of points to consider:

- **Make sure the site is based more on text than graphics.** Every picture tells a story, but it doesn't as far as the search engines are concerned. Even if the image or graphics is composed of all text, Google can't read it so it's ineffective for SEO purposes.

- **Keep your text to between 200 and 600 words.** Any fewer than 200 words and you might not have enough to get your point across, and any more than 600 and it becomes too much of a chore to read. From the SEO standpoint, Google loves more words as it's easier to extract how useful the information is to the visitor, and that's the most important attribute of modern search.

The Bio or About Page

This doesn't have to be your entire life's story. In fact, it's better that it's not. Leave the total history for the bio in your press kit. Two or three paragraphs that gives someone the overall picture of who you are and what you stand for is enough, with a link to the full bio if someone needs more info.

The Contact Page

It's hard to believe how many people overlook this section. Make sure that this link in very obvious. If people can't contact you, they can't book you. Make it easy for them and include not only your email address, but a phone number as well if you're not famous, since some people still prefer to just pick up the phone to make contact.

TIP: *If you don't want people to call your personal phone, then get a Google Voice number, which will stay with you forever and dial any and all phones that you'd like.*

The Subscribe Page

As we talked about in the Chapter 2, the mailing list is the second most important part of your strategy, that's why it's especially important that your sign-up section is prominently displayed on every page (see Figure 4.1). The reason why is that you never know when someone will enter your site from a page other than your home landing page. You can't always be sure that they'll find their way back to the page that has the sign-up links, so just make it easy for them to sign up anywhere on your site. We'll discuss email lists more in Chapter 5.

Figure 4.1: The mailing list subscribe section for Linkin Park

The Press Section

It's amazing that so many brands (which includes artists and bands as well as companies) don't have a proper "Press" section on their website that contains all the information that a journalist or blogger might need when writing a story. I speak from personal experience as a writer in that I'm always surprised with what I *can't* find on a typical site, instead of what I can.

Many brands think that just having a list of press releases is enough, but they're sadly mistaken (especially when the releases are not well organized to begin with, which is quite typical). You have to make available anything about your brand that you think a journalist might need, no matter how mundane, because sometimes the smallest item can make the biggest difference in how an article is written.

Here are some of the essential items that every website press section should have:

- **High resolution color and black and white photos that can be used for print.** Yes, print is slowly dying, but it's still with us and can have a huge impact in certain situations. You never know when you, your music, or your merch will get a mention in a newspaper, magazine or book.

- **Low resolution color photos and graphics for websites and blogs.** A picture says a thousand words and you'd rather someone use one of yours on their blog or website than just supplying a link. Make it easy for them, but give them a variety to choose from.

- **Your logo graphic in different resolutions.** It's surprising how often this is overlooked, but it's just as important as your photos and other graphics.

- **A biography.** Maybe you have an "About Us" or "About Me" section on the website or blog, but a more complete bio, or even a link to it from the press section, makes finding background info about you, your band or company a lot easier for the writer. The easier it is to find, the more likely it will be used.

- **Quotes from the media.** Great quotes about you or your product are also big with writers, since it adds credibility. Limit the quotes to those that are unique though. Ten quotes that all say the same, "You're the greatest," have a lot less impact than one, but it's OK to use several if they say the same thing in totally unique ways.

- **Links to any interviews.** Include links to any interviews that you might have done, either audio, video or just text. No need to post the entire interview on your site as a writer will probably not read it unless he needs some additional facts that he can't find anywhere else.

- **Scans of just three or four of your best press clippings**. Once again, less is more. Ten press clippings that say the same thing tend to actually diminish credibility. Three or four seems about the right number to have in order to give the writer sufficient information.

- **PDFs of adverts, promo flyers and posters.** This has a dual purpose in that its additional info for the writer but can also be used virally by fans. Many "superfans" will print these out and distribute them in their area if asked.

- **Web ready graphics and banners in a variety of sizes**. If you're doing any online campaigns (either advertising or fan-based viral), these can make it quite easy to be up and running in no time since everything is readily available.

- **Press releases.** These are only helpful for a writer if they contain enough background information on a particular subject so details are important. It's also easier for a writer if they're grouped by type (personnel, products, events, etc.) instead of by date.

- **Videos**: You need multiple types of videos - interview elements with the artist or entire band, and if it's a band, individual interviews as well, your most recent music videos, any music video that you consider a "hit," and a clip of a song from a show. It's best to make two versions available - one with smaller web-ready files, and if you're an act that's breaking nationally, another version that's available in hi-res.

- **Music**: Your songs can probably be found online already, but make it easy for whomever is reading by adding links so they can effortlessly find them. If you've done music for commercials or a soundtrack for a movie or television, include that as well but be sure that you have the right to do so before you post it.

- **Web Links**: Be sure to include links to any social media presence that you have on the web such as a Facebook fan page, Instagram page, blog, Twitter, ReverbNation page, etc.

- **Fan Endorsements**: If you have rabid fans that do crazy things like paint themselves up with your logo, get tattoos of your likeness on their backs, or are just super enthusiastic, that could make for an interesting video clip or picture. Just make sure that the fans (three or four is all you need) are completely enthusiastic and really special or this element isn't worth pursuing.

TIP: If you use any endorsement from a fan, be sure to get written permission that it's okay to use it in any form, anywhere.

It's a fact that the easier you make it for a writer or an editor, the more likely you'll get covered. Having these tools easily available will increase your chances of getting media coverage.

By the way, I don't believe in making this info available solely to writers. Make it available to everyone as it can lead to unforeseen viral opportunities. Just keep it up to date (I know how difficult that is, but you've got to try), and your press section will be good to go.

The Booking Info Section

If you're generating some buzz in your local scene, make sure that if an agent or promoter does check out your band that you have pertinent information available on your website for them. Create a "Bookings," "Book Me," or "Book My Band" section on your website, which can be similar to an online press kit, but instead includes specific additions like:

- **Statistics** about the number of newsletter subscribers, Facebook fans and Twitter followers you have. Remember that your social media presence is now taken into consideration by most bookers and promoters, as it's a vital part of their marketing too.

- **Average attendance** for your shows. Are you regularly selling out 50 ,100, or 500-seat venues? Make sure to include it.

- The **markets and venues** that you play in.

- A **photo gallery** with lots of quality live photos, including any that include crowds in packed venues.

- **Good quality live videos** meaning good video quality, good audio quality, packed rooms, and minimal audience talking. Audience sing-a-longs are always worth including as well.

- A **stage plot** of how your gear is normally set up.

- A typical **set list,** if you're a cover band.

- **Quotes from the media** that mention your live show.

- **Quotes from venue bookers**.

- **Quotes from fans** about your live shows.

Other than that, you should always blog and tweet about your live shows, which we'll discuss in Chapters 7 and 11. Post about the turnout, the crowd reaction, and post plenty of pics and live video whenever you can. All of this will help create the impression that you're a hard-working band that takes their live shows seriously.

The Social Media Connections

It's so easy to add links and buttons for Facebook, Twitter, YouTube and almost any other social network you can think of these days. You're missing a great opportunity for increased social interaction and an expanded audience if they're not included.

There are actually two types of icons; those that connect the visitor directly to your social media page, and sharing icons that make it easy for a reader to share the content with their own social media friends and followers.

One easy way to add social media buttons to your site is with something called niftybuttons.com. Just go the site, choose a set of icons, copy the URLs of each of your social pages, then paste it into the slots at niftybuttons. The HTML code is then generated for each of your buttons that you can copy and paste into your website code.

TIP: Most social networks also have a way to generate the code for a number of different social icon versions as well.

The Sitemap

Every website should have a sitemap, which is basically like an office building's directory in that it lists all the pages of your website in one place. Once again, it serves a dual purpose in that it's a last resort item for someone who can't find something on your website (hopefully the navigation is designed so this doesn't happen), and also the bots that the search engines send out love them, which can raise your search engine ranking.

Another advantage is that if your site has a lot of pages, chances are some of them are obscure and don't get much traffic. The sitemap will allow the search engines to index them, which suddenly makes them available to a search.

TIP: Some website development software will automatically generate a sitemap.

Cross-Browser Compatibility

Even though you may love Chrome as your main web browser, there's still a big part of the world that uses Safari, Firefox, Opera, Microsoft Edge, and to a lesser degree these days, Internet Explorer, not to mention their equivalents on iOS and Android operating systems for mobile. That's why it's important that your site is checked on every platform before it goes live to make sure that it appears as you expect it to.

One of the problems is that each browser displays a site slightly differently, so there will always be discrepancies. The trick is to make sure that they're not so major as the look and feel entirely breaks down on one browser while it looks fine on the others. Browser compatibility issues are just one of the many "pleasures" of website development that continue to vex designers everywhere that will probably never go away.

Web Optimized Images

Site load time can be critical to the user experience, which is why so much attention is taken to optimize the images on any site. As an image file size gets larger, it becomes slower to load, which is why ideally most images are kept well below 100kB in size. A good size to aim for is around 50k.

Optimization is a trade-off between image quality and a small file size. At some point, the image quality will suffer as the file size is decreased. Finding the ideal point is where the image detail remains sharp but the file size is sufficiently small. Here are some things to consider when optimizing the images for your site.

- **Make sure that the resolution of the graphic is set to 96 dpi.** 300 dpi is the standard for print (although it can go as low as 150), but that's overkill on a computer monitor. Newer monitors display at 96dpi, so that should be your target resolution (you can go as low as 72, but it won't look good on modern hi-res monitors), but anything higher currently provides no advantage and just makes the file larger.

- **Save your graphics in a jpg, png or gif format.** Any other format may not display and natively will have a file size that's too large for a quick download.

- **Decrease the number of colors to 32**. Most color graphics won't lose all that much even when decreased from a million colors, yet it can make a big difference in file size.

- **Decrease the quality to an acceptable level.** Sometimes the difference between a jpeg quality level of three and ten is so small that you can hardly tell, yet it makes a big difference in the file size.

TIP: File sizes are cumulative to a page. Remember that seven 100kB images equals 700kB, which will load much slower than if they all were half that.

Website Killers To Avoid

Here are a number of practices that are guaranteed to turn off your visitors. You know what they are yourself because you probably encounter them on other sites every day, but that doesn't mean you should emulate a bad practice. Not only do many of the following aggravate site visitors, but they can mean site death when it comes to search engine optimization. If you want fans to find you, make sure these are avoided.

1. A "splash" page. A splash page is an opening page with a movie or flash animation and no information. The whole "Enter Here" thing is so Web 1.0. There's no info for a search engine to grab and your visitors hate them. Avoid at all costs.

2. Flash animation. It looks cool, but sometimes people just want some info and not cartoons. Search engines can't read any of the info in a Flash movie so they're a waste of time and money. iPhones and iPads can't display Flash, and most people hate it these days anyway.

3. Frames. Again, so Web 1.0. Sites with frames went out a long time ago. Get with the times and dump these babies.

4. Pop-ups. It doesn't matter where they come from or if they're selling something or not, everyone hates them.

5. Pull-down boxes for navigation. Designers love them, visitors hate them, search engines can't read them. If your site isn't that complex, stay away if you can.

6. Dead links. This is just poor website quality control. It happens to everyone at some point, but remember that both search engines and visitors hate them.

7. All graphics and not much text. Search engines love text. Visitors love text. Pictures are nice, but use them in moderation.

What Visitors Hate

Technology marches on, and as we know, the pace seems to get faster and faster all the time. The problem is, we all have to keep up in order to both stay relevant and keep our fans engaged. Now comes some research courtesy of getsharesquare.com (a site that helped to mobilize your site, but has unfortunately since closed) that's an eye opener in terms of what visitors really hated about artist's websites.

- 33% of the survey respondents said their most frequent complaint about an artist site was text that was so small that it required zooming.

- 31% stated their biggest complaint was video content that was broken or unavailable.

- 28% said they hated when buttons or links were too small to click.

- 20% hated when streaming music was broken or unavailable.

- 17% complained that recent news and upcoming event info was difficult to find.

- 29% said that they missed the ability to exchange an email address for free content.

- 25% said they really missed the ability to download an artist's song.

- 21% complained that they couldn't purchase tickets or merch directly from the website.

This is a fascinating report in that it indicates that a lot more commerce could be done if only artists would pay more attention to their websites. Many artists take their site for granted, but it should be the main point where all of your fan contact is directed, since it's the one portal online that you have total control of.

Setting Up A Quick Website

It used to be that you needed someone with either the HTML coding skills or the ability to drive an in-depth program like Adobe Dreamweaver in order to develop your website, select and claim you domain name, and select a hosting service to host your site. On top of the that, if your website developer wasn't much of a graphic designer, then you needed to hire one as well and hope that both parties integrate well together. All that has changed thanks to a number of online web development sites that make things a lot easier to get a site up and running.

Today sites like Wix, Weebly and Squarespace, among others, provide everything from clearing domain names, providing hosting, and creating a website easier than ever. These sites provide a number of modern looking templates along with drag-and-drop modules, so there's no need for programming. It does help if you have a graphic designer to create some great images, but that's something that you'll need anyway for branding, promotional material and maybe packaging. The sites are also very reasonably priced from as little as $4 per month, although the lower priced accounts also feature ads. You'll probably want to jump up to the next level at around $10 per month, which is still a bargain.

The best thing about website development sites like these are that they enable you to make changes quickly. Find a mistake? You can change it in literally the time it took to read this. Want to update where you'll be playing? It can be done in a flash. The speed of the updates is what endears many to using these services.

Another alternative is to use a blogging site like Wordpress as the basis for your website. We'll discuss the pros and cons of this in the Chapter 11 about blogs, but I personally prefer one of the dedicated site builders as they're built for the job and a lot easier to get your site online.

Be aware that the more complex your site is, the more time it will take to get up and running. I created a version of my site (bobbyowsinski.com) on Weebly and it has over a hundred pages. This took the better part of week to put together, so make sure you set aside enough time. That said, if you only need five or six pages and you have the graphics ready, you can be online in an hour or so.

Website SEO Techniques

As stated before, SEO (search engine optimization) is the process of designing or fine-tuning your site so that it appears friendly to Google and the other search engines. There are a number of techniques for this, but let's begin with the basics.

Meta Tags

Hidden within the HTML coding of your site is information that search engines look at that we're normally not aware of. In other words, it's information about the information on the site, which is the definition of metadata. We call this kind of metadata "meta tags" and the most important of them are the title tag, description tag, and keywords tag, but there are also several other less important ones that we won't get into.

You don't have to be an HTML programmer to use these, as most of them will be easily available to you when designing a site, although each site development app displays them differently. What's important is that you use them correctly.

Placing Your Name In The Title Tag

The Title tag is the name of the web page. Your website has a title (using "theUnsigned" is our example), but each page on your site also has it's own title, and it's best to make sure it also has your name in it. For instance, if you have a contact page, a title that simply says "Contact" wouldn't be sufficient. The best would be "Contact The Unsigned" or "The Unsigned Contact Info." Likewise, if you have a press page, a title of simply "Press" doesn't cut it while "The Unsigned Press" does. Figure 4.2 shows how the title of my book page, "Bobby Owsinski's Books," shows up in the tab of the browser.

Figure 4.2: Site title in page URL and title

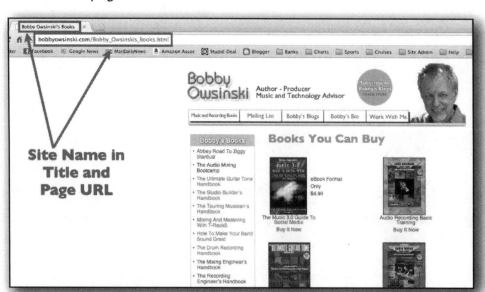

Placing Your Name In The Description

The Description is invisible text that tells the search engines what you're site is all about. When you do a Google search, this is the text that comes up describing your page. Just to show you how this works, if you look below in Figure 4.3 and 4.4, you'll see the description for a site on Google, yet when you look at the site itself, you don't see that same description anywhere on the page.

Figure 4.3: The Gibson site description as seen during a Google search

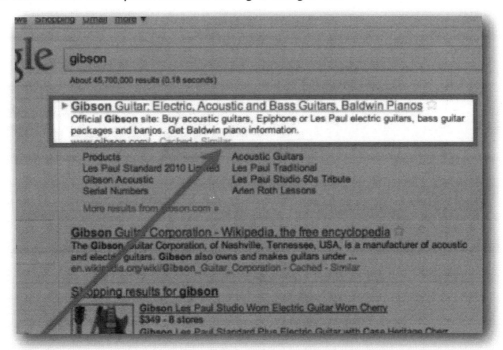

Both Google and Bing will fill the description in for you if you don't create one, but then you're at their mercy as to what they pick off the page. For that reason, you're better off creating one yourself.

The advantage of the description is that search engines use it to help with the search rankings. By making sure that your name is included (as in Figure 4.3 where it says "Official Gibson site"), it makes your search ranking stronger.

Figure 4.4: The description isn't seen on the Gibson site itself

---

TIP: *One caution when creating a description, it must be less than 155 characters, but it's best to stay under 66 to be sure it's all displayed. Also be sure not to use any quotes (" "), since that will stop the description from appearing from that point onward.*

Placing Your Name In The Text Body

Pages that have between 200 to 600 words of text tend to rank better in a search than a page that has less copy and mostly graphics. One of the reasons is that copy gives you a chance to place your name in the text, which again is very strong from an SEO (search engine optimization) standpoint.

The key is to not have the name appear too much though. The ideal amount seems to change all the time, but it's generally acknowledged that two to three percent seems about right. That means that with 200 words of text, your name should only appear four to six times at most. Anything more and it might appear to the search engine as "keyword stuffing" and you'll actually be penalized with a lower search ranking.

Keywords

One upon a time keywords were a big deal to search engines but they've become less of a factor in recent years. Just like with the description, the keywords are invisible to the reader of the site and are only read by the search engines. The problem is that only Bing now bothers with them at all and even then it's only to detect spam.

The best option these days is to restrict them to only five at most, then make sure that they relate to what's on your page. In other words, if you think you sing like Chris Martin of Coldplay but your page has no mention of either Chris Martin or Coldplay, then don't use them as keywords. If you do, you can get penalized again for having keywords that don't relate to your page.

By the way, keywords don't necessarily mean a single word like "music," "guitar," etc. They refer to phrases as well, which are much stronger in that they better target an audience. For instance, "12 string guitar" is much stronger than just "guitar," and "Cleveland 12 string guitar" is better still, because it targets the audience even more.

The Importance Of Anchor Text

Many artists and bands (and even web designers who should know better) fail to realize the importance of *anchor text*. What is anchor text? It's the highlighted text that you use as a link to another site or page. The reason why it's important is that these words can determine your page ranking when someone does a search, since they carry more weight with Google than the other text on the page.

Here's an example of bad use of anchor text (forgive the gratuitous plug):

"To read my Music 3.0 Blog, <u>click here</u>."

"Click here" doesn't mean anything in terms of search. Do you think anyone will ever search for "click here?" Well, someone might (actually there are near 9 billion results on Google), but where do you think you'll rank? Even if you luck out and somehow wind up on page 50, you're still so far back in the search results that it won't do you any good.

A better use of the anchor text would be:

"Click here to read my Music 3.0 Blog."

"Music 3.0 Blog" makes much better anchor text and will take advantage of the way Google weights copy text. You can use your band name, a song title, or anything else that's relevant to get the best results, but a relevant keyword or keyword phrase is always the best. Just remember, anything is better than "click here."

Site Speed

Google has over 200 criteria for site ranking, but one major factor that it considers is how fast your site loads. The reason? Users love fast sites, and fast sites have a higher engagement that slow sites. Google measures the speed in two different ways:

- How a page responds to the Googlebot that crawls the web

- The load time as measured by the Google Toolbar

The Value Of A Fast Page Load

We live in a very impatient world and that impatience could cost you fans, users or sales. A study created by the OnlineGraduateProgram.com found a number of startling facts about our desire for online speed:

- 1 in 4 people abandon a web page if it takes more than 4 seconds to load.

- 50% of mobile users abandon a page if it doesn't load in 10 seconds.

- 40% of mobile shoppers will abandon an e-commerce site that doesn't load in 3 seconds.

- Amazon estimates that it could lose up to $1.6 billion a year because of as little as a 1 second web page delay.

This means that you can't count on the ever expanding bandwidth of your visitors for your site to load quickly, you still must optimize it for speed, because tenths of a second count more than ever. This is one of the reasons to get a pro to build your website so you can be sure to get efficient, streamlined code. Page loading has become so much more than slimmed down graphics files these days.

TIP: *Make sure all of your graphic files are small (30kB to 50kB is about right), and keep any video hosted on YouTube or Vimeo so it all loads fast. Google's too smart for even the smart SEO guys, so play by the rules and don't try to game the system.*

Content Relevance

All that being said, relevance is still the number one factor for site ranking. What is relevance? When the site name, metadata, and text copy of the site all match in relevancy to a search. For instance, if the site name is "JeffBeckTributeBand.com," but the site really tries to sell you insurance, there's not much relevancy there and it will be penalized as a result. Even if the JeffBeckTributeBand.com site is trying to sell tickets to Jeff Beck shows, it's still not about a Jeff Beck tribute band. As a result, even though it's more related, it's still not especially relevant to someone who's searching for a Jeff Beck tribute band.

The point is to make sure that everything about the page relates to one another, in other words, the title, description, copy and keywords are all about the same thing.

easuring Your Backlinks

Backlinks are links to your site on other websites. They're one of the best ways to improve your search engine ranking, so the more you have, the better. They're also a great way to find out exactly what people are saying about you as well. Here's a cool way for you to check those backlinks.

Go to the query window in Google and type "links:yoursite.com" (excluding the quotes) and you'll see all of the backlinks to your site. Here's an example for my main bobbyowsinski.com site below in Figure 4.5.

This method isn't perfect by any stretch of the imagination because, by Google's own admission, it doesn't show all the links to your site, doesn't give you the links in any kind of order, and isn't necessarily up to date. That said, it does give you an idea of who likes you enough to link to you.

Figure 4.5: Using the links operator

TIP: Make sure there isn't a space between the links operator and your website name. In other words, it should be (using my own site as an example) links:bobbyowsinski.com

The Importance Of Deep Links

Usually most bands and artists always provide a link to the home page of their site in any correspondence or social network post. Of course this is better than no link at all, but it might not be the best strategy. According to many SEO gurus, there's now some evidence that "deep linking" can bring you a higher Google ranking by also providing some value to the person following the link as well.

Deep linking is any link on your site that's not your home page *and* has the appropriate information. For example, if you have your picture taken with Katy Perry, it's better for both you and your visitors if you link them directly to the page that has that picture, rather than sending them to your homepage which does not, and forcing them to dig down through your links to find the correct page that displays you and Ms. Perry. Not only is this annoying, but you can get penalized with a lower search ranking by Google for providing a less than perfect user experience as well.

A better strategy might be to mention the picture and provide a direct link to a separate dedicated subpage with the picture, complete with the story behind the picture (don't skimp on the copy - 150 to 300 words is about right), the appropriate metadata (your name, Katy Perry, the place where the picture was taken, etc.), and the appropriate keyword phrases (your name, Katy Perry, the place where the picture was taken, etc.) baked into the copy at about a rate of about 2% (that's about six times or so for each keyword phrase for 300 words). If you use the keywords more frequently, Google may penalize you for "keyword stuffing," and your search ranking can suffer.

Seems like a lot of work, and it is. It's especially difficult to design copy around keywords. I'm a writer with a lot of words under my belt and I still find it hard, but it's worth it if it helps raise your visibility.

What you're aiming for is a lot of backlinks to your deep link, which will raise your ranking and visibility even more.

TIP: Don't forget to submit this subpage to the various search engines and directories, but remember that the subpage has to be able to stand on its own merit or the entire exercise probably isn't worth it. If it takes the visitor only a few seconds to read the copy, then you don't have sufficient stickiness for it to be any benefit to you.

The User Experience

Probably the biggest thing that any search engine looks for these days is the overall user experience of the website. That is, does the site contain the information that the user was looking for in the search. Was it easy to find once he got there? Was it relevant to the search and the SEO provided? Were there misspellings or dead links?

While you can fine-tune your site using all of the above techniques, if the experience is poor once the visitor hits your site, it's all for nothing as Google has algorithms that will actually measure that experience and penalize you with a lower search ranking when it's not a good one. That's why its best not to try anything underhanded in order to try to game the system when it comes to SEO. Google will find out in a flash and penalize you for it.

Website Measurement Techniques

What's the use of having all these great promotional tools unless you can measure how effective they are? As stated previously, in traditional advertising it's long been held that 50% of an advertising campaign works, you just don't know which 50%. That's no longer true online since so much can now be measured, in some cases much more granularly than ever before.

Four Free Website Audience Measurement Tools

There are all sorts of website audience measurement tools now available, but believe it or not, some of the free ones do a great job. While you can get traffic information from your website provider, here are four free measurement tools that can be used as a sort of second opinion when needed.

1. StatCounter: This is by far my favorite measurement tool. StatCounter provides a suite of measurements far more detailed than what you get from your ISP, like the visitor's entry and exit page, where the visitor recently came from, the keywords used to find the site, the time spent on the site, the number of return visits, and location information detailed enough that you can almost see into the visitor's house (see Figure 4.6).

You just place a piece of invisible code on your website or blog and away you go. The free version of StatCounter only remembers the info for your last 500 visitors, and anything beyond that requires a monthly fee, but what you get in the free version is still very useful.

Figure 4.6: A granular look at a StatCounter visitor map

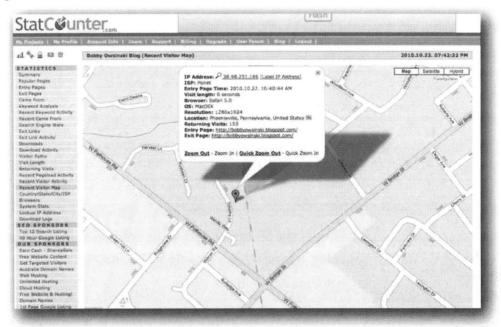

2. 33Across: Another tool that requires that you insert some invisible code, 33Across differs from just about anything else in that it measures how many copies of text or graphics were made from your site or blog (see Figure 4.7). In other words, if someone copies a piece of text from your site and inserts it on another site or blog, 33Across knows about it, and then can track how many visits came to your site from that copied piece. What's more, you can also program it to insert a Creative Commons license warning when someone copies and pastes your content. The analytics are difficult to decipher sometimes, but it's certainly a cool and useful tool.

3. Google Analytics: There's no code to paste into your website with Google Analytics. You just register your site or blog, then leave the rest to Google. You get somewhat the same information as with StatCounter, but you also get some trending information that's very useful. It's also one of the most widely used measurement tools around.

4. Quantcast: This is considered by many to be the de facto standard for measuring web audiences, and is preferred by companies like MTV, Time, Gawker and Fox among many others. The information provided includes traffic, demographics, geography, site affinity and categories of interest. Like some of the other services, it requires that you install some invisible code on your site for measurement.

There are a ton of paid measurement tools out there, but why spend any money until you really need to? These four will get you started and take care of most of your measurement needs for quite a while.

TIP: It's an interesting quirk that each measurement service will provide somewhat different data, which is okay if you expect it to happen up front. It's best to average the results and watch for trends in order to make the best use of what they offer.

Website Performance Metrics

When it comes to measurement, one of the things that can happen is that it's easy to be almost overwhelmed by the data that a measurement tool can provide. Here's a way to interpret that data in order to understand just how successful your website really is. Thanks to Hubspot for the definitions.

1. Unique visitors: That's the total number of individual visitors to your site during a specific period of time, not counting repeat visits by the same individual. Obviously, if this number continues to increase, you're doing well.

2. New versus repeat visitors: This is a comparison of your unique visitors versus the number of visitors who came back more than once. Although it's great to have repeat visitors (and you really need them), a rate higher than 50% means that you're probably not growing your audience quickly enough.

3. Traffic sources: This is a breakdown of the specific sources of traffic to your website. There are two: *Organic traffic* comes from a link found on a search engine results page. *Referral traffic* comes from a link on another website. This tells you how well your search engine optimization is doing. A referral level of about 30% is what you're looking for.

4. Referring URLs: This measurement shows the specific, non-search engine URLs that send traffic directly to your site. They represent the inbound links that are crucial for boosting your site's search engine rankings, and tell you which sites or bloggers are linking to your site and what type of content they tend to like.

5. Most/least popular pages: This is a comparison of the pages on your site that receive the most and least traffic that tells you which kind of content your visitors prefer.

6. Conversion rate: This is the percentage of visitors to your site who take a desired action, such as purchasing a product or filling out a lead generation form. This tells you how well you're converting leads into fans or customers.

7. Bounce rate: This is the percentage of new visitors who leave your site almost immediately after arriving with no other interaction. A high bounce rate means that your visitors don't find your pages particularly compelling, or they may be looking for something other than what you're offering.

Interpreting the above metrics should give you some idea of just how well your site is performing. Hubspot has a bit more on all of these points, plus a few more, if you're interested.

Summing It Up

There's been a lot written in this chapter about how to create the best website possible, but it all can be broken down to just the essentials. Here it is:

- Have an easy to remember site name

- Use the same name in the URL, title, description and first paragraph

- Use 200 to 600 words of copy per page

- Have a mailing list signup section

- Have a press kit section

- Have a contact section

- Have social media connection buttons

- Back links are one of the keys to high search engine rankings

- Don't use more than five keywords maximum, but make sure that they relate to the content on the page

- Refresh your content as often as possible

TIP: *Remember that it's best if everything that's on your site is aimed at providing your visitor with the best experience possible. This will cause your site to rank high in a search, making it easier for people to find you.*

Creating Your Mailing List

5

Perhaps the second most powerful marketing tool you have after your website is your email list. The reason is that anyone who subscribed has not only given you permission to communicate directly with them, they're hoping that you do since they're interested in whatever you have to say and promote. Because of this conscious opt-in, the email newsletter is the most direct link to your fans and clients.

Mailing List Overview

Before we cover the details of getting a mailing list and newsletter up and running, let's take a quick overview of the world of email and how it influences our everyday lives.

Email Is Not Dead

It appears that reports of email's demise are untrue, according to a recent survey of 2,200 adults in the US and UK by Harris Interactive. Despite the rise of social networking, we're still addicted to it and we're not letting go. Here's what the survey found:

- 72% in the US and 68% in the UK check their email during their time off.

- 19% of Americans check email in bed (21% men and 16% women)

- 50% check their email while on vacation and during off-days

- 46% of American respondents check their email to ease their workload

- 37% are afraid that they'll miss something important

- 27% check work email at home because it's expected of them

- 26% check email on vacation because that's the only way they can handle the volume

While it may be popular to think that the use of email is declining in favor of social networks, the fact is that email is still a huge part of our everyday lives. The problem is that we get so much of it that an email newsletter may have a hard time rising above the rest of the email noise. That said, the data shows that people do check their mail and it's still important to them. It's up to you to send it.

Four Reasons Why Your Email List Is So Important

While the trend is to think that email is on the decline when it comes to communicating with friends, fans, clients and business associates as social networks like Facebook rise in popularity, it's a lot more important than you think when it comes to promotion. Here are four reasons why.

1. You control the message. Your email list is one of the most powerful tools you can have because you control the message, and if done well, it can feel a lot more personal than communicating via Facebook or Linkedin or any of the other popular networks. You control the information, the look, the marketing and the promotion in a way that's not possible in any social network, since each social network has its own look and feel as well as a terms-of-service agreement that can limit what you can say and do.

2. Your message is consistent. Although the ability to control the message is important, being able to control the *consistency* of that message is even more so. For most artists and musicians today, the problem becomes how to effectively communicate with all of your "friends" and contacts across various networks, because social networks are a closed environment by nature. That means that you have a set of friends on Facebook, another set on Twitter, and a different set on another network like Pinterest or Instagram. As a result, the look and feel will be inconsistent because of the nature of the various networks. If you're not consistent in your presentation, you're not controlling the message.

3. It's a memory prompt. One of the best things about a newsletter is that it reminds fans or former clients who you are. If a person hasn't been following you on a social network and therefore doesn't see any of your regular posts, that newsletter in their email box jogs their memory and reminds them you're around. It doesn't take long to drift from the public consciousness, and an email prevents that from happening.

4. You can measure its effectiveness. One thing that email can provide that social networks don't do nearly as well is sophisticated measurement. With email we know when a newsletter was opened, if it was opened more than once (even if it's reopened again a year later), how long it was read, if any of the links were clicked, and if it was passed along to anyone else, among many other measurements. Obviously your personal email app on your computer can't do these things, and it can't easily reach out to thousands of people as well. That's why you need a service like Constant Contact, Mailchimp, or iContact, all of which also have the added convenience of constantly cleaning the list of bounces and outdated addresses.

Using A Mailing List Service

When I wanted to send one of my first email newsletters to a list of only about 1200 (which seemed large at the time but is really tiny in grand scheme of email lists), I was astounded to find that my Internet Service Provider (ISP) wouldn't allow me to send to more than 100 addresses simultaneously from my business account. That meant that I had to split my list up into 12 batches, which made the job take a lot longer than it should have. After a number of calls to my Internet service provider at the time, I discovered that just about every ISP limits the number of email addresses that can be attached to an email in an attempt to keep spam in check, yet I knew that there were companies that sent emails to millions of addresses at a time every day. How did they do it?

That's when I found out about email service providers or ESPs. ESPs have an agreement with the various Internet service providers to make sure that their customers aren't what we would consider spammers.

While the odd few may push up against those boundaries, ESPs go to great lengths to make sure that you don't fall into that category by constant checking spam reports and large email address imports, then making you personally verify that your lists are opt-in and not purchased or just skimmed from a forum.

That said, the only limit to how many addresses you can send to hinges on how much money you want to spend, since almost all ESPs work on the same principle - the greater the number of email addresses, the more it costs.

ESPs are way more useful than just providing basic email delivery however, and are definitely worth the money. Among some of the other things they do are:

- clean your list for you, which means they automatically delete any old non-existent or invalid addresses (you have to do it manually if you use your personal email app, which is a big drag time-wise).

- provide a means to measure how well your email did in terms of open rate, click-throughs, pass-alongs, and a lot more.

- provide a means to easily subscribe and unsubscribe to the list (again, this is much more difficult to do manually).

- provide a host of pretty good looking HTML templates that you can use to easily design a professional looking email blast.

- give you a way to easily segment your list so you can target an email blast better.

Most email service providers offer many more services than the main ones mentioned here. In fact, each one offers slightly different features, so it's best to check out a few of them before you make a decision which one's right for you.

An Overview Of Mailing List Service Providers

Here's a list of email service providers to investigate. Each has their pros and cons, so it's best to check every one out thoroughly before you commit. Since most of them also have free 30 day trials, you can try before you buy to see if a particular service is what you're looking for.

As stated above, all of them have a nice selection of professional-looking email templates, but how they're customized is slightly different, so be sure to check that out. Of course, if you already have a web designer that can design a good looking HTML newsletter, the templates won't matter as much to you as the other features.

- Mailchimp.com
- Aweber.com
- Campaigner.com
- Campaignmonitor.com
- Feedblitz
- MyNewsletterBuilder.com
- iContact

- WhatCounts
- Constant Contact
- GetResponse
- Vertical Response
- BenchmarkEmail
- PinPointe
- MyEmma

These are only just a sampling of the popular ESPs available, and you can also find a number of email list review sites that will give you a ranking and allow you to easily compare services.

The Email Subscribe Form

After you've decided upon an ESP, the next step is to get your fans or clients email addresses into a list. There are a number of ways to do this, but first you have to create a list or lists.

Lists

All ESPs allow you to create multiple mailing lists so that you can target a list with a particular email when necessary (see Figure 5.1). For instance, if you're an artist, you may create a separate list for every city that you perform in so you can email only those fans in a particular area, alerting them of your upcoming gig there. Perhaps you play in too many cities for that to be practical, so you might want to segment your lists by region instead. If you're an engineer or producer, you may want a list of past clients and another of potential clients. Maybe you want a separate list for engineering clients and another for production clients. You can have as many lists as you want, and you can choose to send an email to all of them or only one as is appropriate. Also, you can have the same contacts on more than one list, as most ESPs are smart enough to know to only send a single email in the event that you're sending to multiple lists.

TIP: *One recommendation is to set up at least one list that's a "general" catch-all list as well as any other lists you might think you need in the future. Don't worry about naming it, you can always rename it or delete it later, and you can move email addresses freely between lists as well.*

Figure 5.1: A look at my lists on Constant Contact

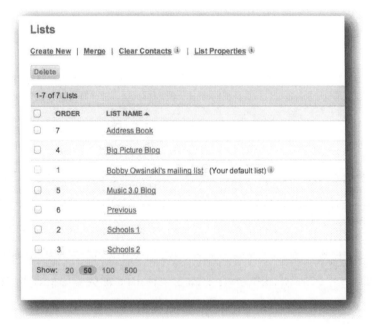

Manual Entry

You've probably collected some email addresses already, and they will make up the bulk of your initial mailing list. All ESPs allow you to manually enter those addresses into any list that you choose in a number of ways. First you can copy and paste the addresses into the appropriate area, making sure there's a comma behind each (some ESPs want you to put each address on a separate line instead of a comma).

You can also enter in a large number of addresses by importing either an Excel file, a CSV file (comma separate value), or a text file. Some ESPs also allow you to import directly from your Gmail or Outlook address books (see Figure 5.2).

Figure 5.2: Manual entry of email addresses

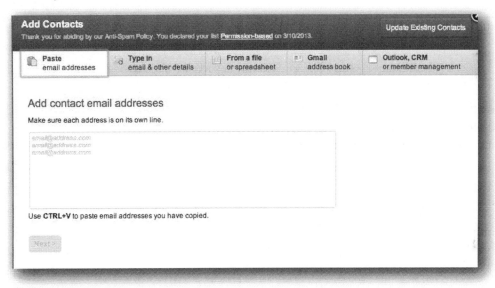

A word of caution about entering or importing a large group of addresses. No ESP wants to accommodate a spammer, since it can endanger their reputation and have them blocked by some ISPs. As a result, ESPs are very nervous if you suddenly show up with a list of 10,000 names, so they ask you to ensure that you haven't purchased the list or gotten it any other way than people personally opting in. In fact, some will send a new opt-in message just to make sure that your imported addresses really want to be on the list.

If you're moving your list from one service to another, this won't be a problem, but if you're harvesting every email address that you've ever come in contact with, it might be. If after your first mailing there are a lot of bounces and spam reports, the ESP may terminate your service. That's why you have to be careful about using a list that you didn't grow organically. Everybody hates spam, so you have to be extra careful that whatever you send isn't perceived as such.

The Subscribe Form

It's all well and good to be able to manually import email addresses, but there's also a way for that to happen automatically when someone decides they want to be on your list. Every ESP has a way for you to generate the code for a sign-up form to put on your website, blog or social media page.

What you have to do is decide how much information that you need for the subscription to take place. Usually this means the email address for sure, but you also might want at least the person's first name so you can address the email personally to him or her (most ESPs will do that automatically for you), the city and the state they're in. You can also ask for a full address, phone number, school and anything else you think might be important, but remember that the more you ask for, the less likely you'll have someone sign up. It's a fact that people become more reluctant to reveal their personal info, and may just decide that the subscription is not worth the trouble.

Take the code that the ESP generates, paste it into the HTML code of your website (or have your webmaster do it), and you'll see something like in Figure 5.3. The last thing you'll have to do is select which list this subscription will go to. That's why I suggest creating a "general" (you can call it whatever you want) list that only collects these emails, although it's also possible to have individual sign-up forms for your website, Facebook page, blog, etc. that each goes to a different list.

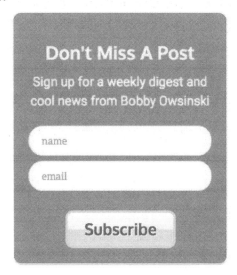

The Welcome Email

When someone subscribes to your email, most ESPs allow you to automatically send a "welcome" email (sometimes called an "Autoresponder") to the new subscriber. This can outline when to expect to receive emails, what's in those emails, or even provide a link to something free in exchange for the email address.

Here's an example of the email that comes from subscribing to my music production blog.

Hi xxx, (name of subscriber)

This is Bobby Owsinski and I just wanted to send you a quick thank you for subscribing to my Music Production Blog list.

This means you'll get a digest every Monday of blog posts from the week before so you'll never miss one.

From time to time I'll also be sending you some interesting items that I think you might find useful as well.

There's absolutely no cost, I think you'll get tons of value from it, and you can unsubscribe at any time.

You might also be interested in checking out my Music 3.0 new music business blog, or checking out some of my online courses as well.

Thanks again for subscribing. If you have any questions or comments, feel free to contact me.

Bobby

The Double Opt-In

Some ESPs encourage something called a "double opt-in." An opt-in means that you've intentionally signed up to receive the email newsletter and weren't put on the list without your knowledge. A double opt-in means that instead of directly receiving a welcome email, you receive a second chance to either opt-in or decline first. That means that if you went to a website and signed-up your friend, your friend would get an email that basically says "Are you sure you're the one that opted-in, and do you still want to do this?"

ESPs especially love double opt-ins because it provides a higher level of security that your list won't be used for sending spam. The problem is that it also gives your subscriber another chance to change his mind in that if he doesn't take action to confirm his subscription, his original opt-in is no longer valid.

When People Subscribe

It's great when you do have someone sign-up to your list, but keep the following in mind:

- The highest unsubscribe rate occurs among those who have been subscribers for less than 10 days.

- Unsubscribes tend to happen within the first few emails after someone subscribes.

On the other hand:

- The highest click-through-rate (CTR) is with those who have been subscribers for less than 10 days.

- Sending emails directly after a person subscribes is a very effective sales tool, since they're paying close attention.

That's why it's best to have a special email newsletter ready for new subscribers that tells all about your music and merch and where to get them. This is done using the "AutoResponder" part of your ESP. In fact, most ESPs allow you to program multiple autoresponder emails so the new subscriber can be contacted at regular intervals. This is the perfect strategy to keep them in the fold and strike while the iron is hot.

Crafting A Successful Email Newsletter

There's a lot of thought that goes into creating a newsletter. If your title doesn't attract attention, the email may not get opened. If the content is weak, the next one might not get opened, or worse yet, the person could unsubscribe. You could have a great offer that no one acts on because it's presented poorly or visually buried. Let's take a look at the elements of a great newsletter.

The Objective

Sending out a newsletter for the sake of sending one out isn't a good strategy. There has to be a good reason for you to communicate with your subscribers. Don't forget, they gave you permission to contact them in the first place. It's up to you not to soil that agreement. Before you decide to send any newsletter, ask yourself these three questions:

- **What is this email about?** Are you informing your subscribers about the latest news? Are you trying to promote something? Is this an announcement of some kind? Decide what your email is about, then keep that as your central focus.

- **Why do my subscribers care?** Is this something they would be sorry about missing? Is it something they want to participate in? What's in it for them?

- **What do they do about it?** Do you want them to pass something along? Buy something? Come to a show? Stay informed about your life? Whatever it is, be sure to ask them to do it.

The Subject Line

The subject line is extremely important because if done well, it entices the person that receives the email to actually open it. Remember that we live in a world of spam, and people get so much email every day that if the title doesn't immediately register with them as important, it's in the trash.

It's important to keep your subject line to 55 characters or less. Most email clients that people use cut the subject line off after that many anyway, so keep your subject line short and to the point - five or six words max.

Above all, don't use something like "Hey" or "Yo" alone in the subject line. That has spam written all over it and chances are your open rate is going to be near zero. Put some thought into the subject line and you'll be rewarded with a high open rate.

Also remember that using a first name in subject line grabs attention. Something like this:

"Hey Jeremy! News From The Unsigned Band"

Most ESPs will allow this, as long as you've connected the first names in your sign-up form. Testing shows that the response rates go up 50 to 70% or more when a first name is included. Remember that "Come to my show" is too predictable and uninteresting. If it's boring, people won't open or read it, and they won't come to your show.

The Salutation

As in the subject line, first names get attention, so try to use the first name of each person you send your newsletter to. That's why it's also better if you can at least collect the subscriber's first name on the sign-up form. If you have a large number of email addresses without a name, it's probably better to send a separate version of the email to them without a salutation at all, but avoid something that's too generic like "Dear subscriber," which degrades any personal impact that the newsletter might otherwise have. Something like "Greetings from beautiful downtown Burbank (or whatever town or city you want to use)" is a good catch-all that seems personal even if you don't have the subscribers name.

The Copy

The copy is the body of your email where most of the text resides. Here's what to be aware of when composing:

1. What's the news? Part of crafting a quality email is having a clear sense of what exactly the big news is. Your text should focus on the most newsworthy element of your announcement with supporting details (including multimedia links) that clearly lay out why this news is significant. Also, try to make it as timely as possible. There's no sense in focusing the email on something that happened months ago. Stay with the present or the near future.

2. Always give them the basics about the information you're conveying. Reporters call this the "who, what, why, when, where, how" model. If you have a show coming up, do your fans and yourself a favor by providing dates, times, locations, ticket links, a map and lineup of the show. Believe it or not, the majority of artists miss this when they send an email. If you want someone to respond and either come to a show or purchase something, give them all the information they need to do so.

3. Keep it short. Time is your enemy in a newsletter. The longer it takes to read, the less someone wants to read it. It's not that your fans don't care, it's just that either their time or attention span is short, since there's so much else going on at the same time. If you have a good story with good visuals, the newsletter can be quick, succinct, and to the point; all things that make everyone's job easier. The ideal amount of text is around 500 words. You can always add a link to a page on your site with more details.

4. Add some pictures. If your newsletter is all text, it won't be visually appealing. Once again, any hint of boredom and it won't be read entirely.

5. Don't concentrate on too many things. You may have a dozen things going on that you want to convey, but that will mean that the email will increase in length and there will be too many concepts for the reader to focus on. Try to keep it to the most important one or two items per email. You can either send people to a page on your site via a link for more info on the other items, or send another email focusing on a few of them in a week or two.

6. Keep important content above the fold. If your email is long enough that it requires the reader to scroll down to see it all, keep the most important information at the top before the reader has to scroll. This is known as "above the fold" and the concept comes from the newspaper days where the upper half of the page was where the top headline was located. The same idea still applies even in the digital world; keep the most important info at the top of the page.

7. Always be sure there's a link to a place with more info. The link could be to your website, a ReverbNation page, a blog, or anywhere else where the additional info is located. Always give the reader a way to find out more if he wants to.

8. Write without swearing. It may be part of your persona as an artist or band, but not all of your fans or clients like crude language. On top of that, ISPs like Yahoo mail, hotmail, AOL don't like it either, and your message can be directed into the junk box if you're not careful.

Your Call To Action

A "call to action" is when you ask the recipient to do something. Do you want him to come to your site? Come to a show? Buy something? No matter what it is, readers are more inclined to act if you ask them (surprise, surprise). Some typical call to action statements might be "Buy it here," "Order it now," "Click for more info," or even "Send me your comments" links in the email.

One of the things you should be aware of though, if the call to action has too much hype it comes across as selfish or gives the perception that all you want is the reader's money. If it's presented more as information that the reader might like instead of a sales pitch, you'll usually sell more and maintain your good will as well. Another thing to keep in mind is that you should always give before you get. Give the fans something special before you ask them to do something like vote for you in a contest.

Social Media Sharing

Even though you're communicating via an email, social media is still important. Each newsletter should also include links or icons to your social sites so people who aren't yet following you can do so easily, as well as embedded social sharing functions. This allows people to tweet or add your news to their Facebook status. Do this and you've just multiplied your audience.

Your Signature

Make sure to include all of your info in your signature. If people want to contact you, they shouldn't have to go through a game of hide-and-seek to find out how. The very minimum that you should include is your website, your email address, your Facebook page and Twitter address. Don't forget to include your YouTube channel address either.

Legal Requirements

While it may seem that it's entirely up to you about what's contained in your email, be aware that every mass email blast that you send now requires several things by law. These are:

- **Easy opt-out:** You have to provide an easy way for subscribers to unsubscribe if they want. Once a subscriber opts out, you then have 10 days to stop sending them messages (although most expect it to happen immediately), and the unsubscribe option needs to be available for at least 30 days after the e-mail is sent. Most ESPs will automatically remove the address to a "do not send" list if the subscriber chooses to unsubscribe.

- **Identify your topic:** The subject line of your e-mails has to clearly and accurately identify the content of the e-mail. Any misleading or bogus subject lines are construed as spam.

- **Return address:** You have to include a legitimate return email address, as well as a valid postal address. Some ESPs even make you include a phone number. If you don't want people to know your home info (I don't want to broadcast it myself), open up a PO box, and get a Google Voice number if a phone number is required.

- **No email address harvesting:** You can't collect addresses from chat rooms, discussion forums, or blog comments. Once again, people must opt-in and give you permission to send something to them.

- **You can't offer a reward for forwarding:** You can invite subscribers to "forward this newsletter to a friend," but you can't entice them to do so with offers of money, coupons, discounts, awards, or additional entries in a giveaway.

Remember that spam is a serious business. It's not only bad form, but you could be held legally liable as well.

The Best Times To Email

You've finally finished creating your newsletter email and it's time to hit the send button. But is it really? It turns out that the exact day and time that's optimum to send your email has been extensively studied, and thanks to the built-in scheduler now offered by ESPs, you can be sure to have your email sent at the time when it's most likely to be opened.

The Best Day Of The Week For Email Marketing

What's the best day of the week to send your email newsletter? This is a critical decision because if you send it on the wrong day, you'll have fewer of your fans open it. Why? Usually because the timing is bad and their attention is on something else. That's why you want to be sure to pick the right day.

Here's some info from an article on gather.com that analyzes every day of the week as a potential email day. The article drew no conclusions and was able to provide a compelling argument for almost every day except the weekend.

MONDAY: After a long weekend, many email users make it a priority to organize their inboxes. This means there's a good chance that they'll run across your message and open it. The problem is that many consumers don't have the time because Monday is such a busy day as most people have to deal with the work backup from the weekend. If you choose to send an email on Monday, *it's best to do it late in the morning, preferably just before lunch*, as this is when they're more likely to have the time to check their inbox.

TUESDAY: By Tuesday, many consumers have organized their work week and have a little extra time to devote to checking their inbox. Like record releases, I've always felt that Tuesday is the best day to release or send anything. It's usually a slower news day, everyone is over the rush and pent up obligations that Monday brings, and you're not caught up in the business craziness that grows ever more intense as the week progresses.

WEDNESDAY AND THURSDAY: By mid-week people are preparing for the weekend and how they'll spend their personal time. On these two days, they often have a little extra time to spend in their inbox. The problem is that there's still business that needs to be handled and only two days left to get it done. Depending on the recipient, they may hold your message off until next week, or forget about it altogether. If you choose, mid-week to send your email, *keep your marketing message friendlier and less aggressive* as subscribers plan their time off.

FRIDAY: People tend to receive less email on Friday, which in turn, increases the visibility of your message. The problem is that by the time Friday rolls around, some consumers are in such a rush that they may automatically ignore any email that doesn't pertain to their job. If you do choose Friday, *send your message early in the day* so the recipient has more time to read it and take action.

SATURDAY AND SUNDAY: Believe it or not, people do check their inboxes on the weekend, and open rates are 45% higher and click rates 10% higher than the rest of the week. The problem is that by sending emails on Saturday or Sunday, you run the risk of coming off as too intrusive and annoy your subscribers, which is a good reason to avoid the weekend. If you do choose the weekend, limit your mailings to subscribers who are the most responsive on these particular days, especially targeted fans that you want to remind about a gig. I've always found that Saturday was the worst day of the week to send something, while Sunday was one of the best days.

Selecting The Time To Send Your Email

Just like there's a best day to send your newsletter, there's also a definite science behind the time of day to send your emails. It's been studied extensively, most notably by Dan Zarrella and Pure360. Remember that all times are *Eastern Standard Time.*

- **Most opens occur between 5AM and 7AM.** Most people check their email first thing in the morning even before they leave for work. Remember that open rates are as much as 53% higher in the mornings.

- **7AM to 10AM is the next best time for opens.** The second most prevalent email opening time is at the beginning of the working day.

- **10PM to 6AM is an email dead zone.** Most emails sent during this period are ineffective.

Remember that these are trends and might not apply to your particular audience. The best way to proceed is to use these timings as a starting point, then experiment to see if another time works better. It's easy enough to schedule emails to do so, just make sure that you have enough of a sample size before you make any ironclad decisions on exactly what's working.

To sum things up, don't send those promotional emails out without first thinking about the timing. It could mean the difference between your fans reading it or not.

Frequency Of Emails

Now that you've gotten your email lists together and that first email out of the way, the next question always is, "How often should I email?" This basically depends upon how much news you have and what your subscribers expect.

You're probably currently on some sales lists like Buy.com or Ebay Deals where you receive an email every day or even multiple times a day. As you know, you only glance at it at most, stopping if something catches your eye or if you're specifically looking for an item, which probably isn't all that frequently. That's not the fate you want for your email though, as you'd prefer that your readers devour every word.

Here are some rules of thumb on email frequency:

- If you dislike the process of creating an email or just don't have anything to say at the moment, send an email every quarter (three months) just to keep your name in the mind of your fans and clients.

- If you have a fair amount of news that's occurring on a regular basis, an email every month or two can be very effective.

- If you're starting to break out in a big way, you may have enough content for once a week. This is rare for most artists though, and it's hard to constantly come up with enough information that your fans will find interesting.

- It's okay to send an email more frequently or out of sequence if something unexpected happens, like you're nominated for an award, your album is reviewed in a major magazine, or some major event happens. Fans want to hear this, so don't be afraid to send something to alert them.

TIP: For most artists, bands, engineers, producers and music business folks, an email every month or two is about the right frequency, as it's just long enough that your fans don't feel like they're being spammed and not too long before they forget you.

Gig Reminders

Gig reminder emails fall into a different category in that they can be a lot shorter and a lot more frequent. While the email sequence below may seem like a lot of emails, remember that for true fans, you're doing them a favor by keeping them informed, and you're marketing yourself for other things at the same time. A potential reminder strategy is:

- **The day a show is announced or tickets go on sale.** As soon as you know that you're playing at a venue, send out an email. This could be to the entire list if it's announcing a tour, if it's the monthly schedule for a cover band, or if you believe that people will travel to see the show.

- **A week before the show.** Send out a reminder but concentrate more on the band, regarding a new part of the show, new songs, a music video, or something that you want to the fan to see.

- **3 days before the show.** Send out a reminder and include more information about the club and who else is playing.

- **1 day before the show.** Once again, remind the fan about a a different feature of the show or the music that's unique and won't be seen or heard any other way than attending. You can change the headline to "You don't want to miss this," or "See our new show tomorrow night."

- **The day of the show.** Send out a short reminder in the late morning to just the portion of your list in the general area of the club. Use a headline like, "Can you make it tonite?", or "Last chance to buy tickets!"

- **The day after the show**. Send an email with backstage pictures, pictures of meet and greets with fans or just fans in the audience, as well as links to videos. This is a nice shout-out to those that were there, and a prod for those that weren't not to miss you next time you're in town.

Of course, if you're lucking enough to have sold out your show, you won't need to send as many reminders. That said, you might send one headlined "Sold Out!" that either announces another gig or another way for the fan to hear your music or buy your merch. A contest for two last minute tickets (put them on your guest list) also works well.

TIP: In every reminder be sure to include all the pertinent gig information, including the name of the venue, the full address, the phone number, the time you're going on, and other acts on the bill. Consider including a map or a link to one as well.

Artists and bands are sometimes timid about sending out so many gig announcements, but fans that ordinarily would attend really do forget. Remember, you're doing them a favor by reminding them.

TIP: When sending out multiple emails in a short space of time, be sure to continually change the headline and the email format and contents.

Building Your Mailing List

Just like with your social media follows and Likes, building your mailing list takes some work. In general it comes down to the following:

- **Trust in your site.** If your site or social page makes people uncomfortable in any way, chances are they won't give you their email address.

- **An incentive of some kind.** Generally speaking, people don't want to give their address out unless they're get something in return. Don't think about the fact that you're getting their email address, think of what's in it for the fan. He only may care about regular communication, but usually access to something free (an exclusive video, ticket, ebook, article) gets better results.

- **Make it easy by not asking for too much information.** The more info you ask from a potential subscriber, the greater the chance that he'll give up while subscribing. Asking for just an email address gets the greatest response, but adding a first name allows you to include a personal greeting.

- **Cross-promote across social media, business cards, banners, and anywhere else you can think of**. Anywhere you get a chance to mention your email list, do so.

- **Reminders in your content.** Mention your mailing list in any podcasts, blogs, or videos, because sometimes even if it's right in front of them, a reminder is still needed.

Your email list is extremely powerful for communicating, interacting, and promoting to your fans. Put sufficient time and effort into it and you'll be richly rewarded.

Using Facebook For Marketing

6

Facebook launched in February of 2004 and quickly grew into the powerhouse that we know today. While many see it for its flaws, the mere size of the network (over 2 billion users) makes it a social source that can't be overlooked. In this chapter we'll look closer at how to use Facebook not only for promotion, but for increasing your fan base as well.

Facebook By The Numbers

Here's an interesting set of statistics from Facebook itself. A couple of figures jump out, like the almost 5 billion Likes per day, and the fact that the network has zero penetration into China and only 11% into India and 60% in the US. Even with 2 billion current users, that still leaves some room for growth. Check out these facts:

- It's the second most popular visited site on the Internet after Google.

- 66% of active users log on in any given day.

- About 85% of Facebook active daily users are outside the United States.

- An average user spends 700 minutes per month on Facebook.

- More than 5 billion pieces of content are shared on Facebook each day.

- Each day, Facebook Pages have created 5.3 billion fans.

- Each day, 55 million status updates are made on Facebook.

- More than 1.15 billion active users currently access Facebook through their mobile device.

The numbers don't lie, and any one of the above points is enough to make the case to use Facebook. Put them all together and it means that being a part of it is almost mandatory when it comes to social promotion.

Facebook Basics

Before we look at using Facebook for marketing, let's take a look at some of the basics, since there may be a bit of confusion about a few of its features. This is especially the case when it comes to personal versus fan pages, but as you'll see, there are good reasons to have both.

The Difference Between A Personal And Fan Page

There are two kinds of pages that you can have on Facebook; a personal page and a fan/business (they're basically the same) page. They're not interchangeable and each has its own advantages and disadvantages.

The Personal Page

First of all, you can't administrate a fan page unless you have a personal page, so there's no getting around having one unless someone else is administering your fan page for you. The next thing is that the personal page is the best place to stay in touch with family and friends. You can still have fans follow you, but you can segment them using a feature called "Lists." This will allow you to communicate just with the people you wish so you can keep things private if necessary.

To create a new list:

- Click *Friend Lists* under *Explore* on the left side of your News Feed.

- Click *Create List*.

- Enter a name for your list and the names of friends you'd like to add. Keep in mind you can add or remove friends from your lists at any time.

- Click *Create*.

In addition to any lists you create, you'll also see *Smart Lists*. Smart lists are automatically created and stay up-to-date based on profile information you and your friends have in common (ex: work, school, family, city).

Perhaps the two biggest reasons why a personal page is no substitute for a fan page is the fact that a personal page can have a maximum of 5,000 friends, plus you can't access any of the analytics (called Facebook Insights) that are available on a fan page.

Your Facebook Fan Page

The fan page differs from a personal page in that you can have an unlimited number of Likes and access to Facebook analytics, but it also has a number of additional advantages beyond that. These are the things other than the privacy aspect that make a fan page attractive.

- **Pinning posts on the Timeline.** If there's a particular post that you'd like to appear at the top of your timeline, the administrator (hopefully you) can pin it there (see Figure 6.1). This will keep the post at the top of the page for seven days, after which it will return to the date when it was posted. This ensures that everyone will see that particular post for a week, at which time it's probably old news anyway. To pin a post, click on the edit button on the top right of a post.

Figure 6.1: Pinning a post to the Timeline

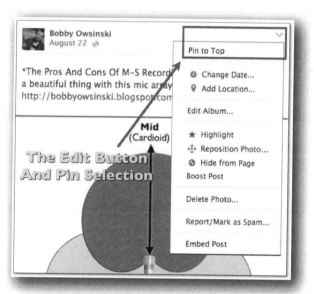

- **A unique experience.** The beauty of a fan page is that each fan gets a different experience. If someone visits your fan page, they also see what their friends are posting about you, even though it's not posted directly on your fan page.

The Cover Graphic

One of the things that you should take the time to do is to upload a cover photo or graphic. This allows you to brand your page beyond your profile picture. Although you can upload any photo and it will expand or contract to fill the space, it's best if you can create one that's 851 x 315 pixels with a file size of less than 100kB (see Figure 6.2). That way it will load quickly and contribute to a better looking user experience.

Facebook has a number of guidelines for your cover photos like:

- It can't have price or purchase information in the photo (like "50% off").

- It can't include a call to action to Like, comment or share with your friends.

- It can't include contact info like web, email or mailing address (there are better places to put this rather than on the cover photo as well).

Figure 6.2: Cover image specs

851 pixels

315 pixels

Less than 100kb

TIP: Make sure that you use a real photo of you for your profile picture, not one of your baby pictures, not an avatar, and not one of a celebrity that's not you. People won't trust either your personal or fan page if they can't trust your profile picture.

When To Start A Fan Page

If you're an artist or band starting out, I don't believe that it's a good idea to jump right in with a fan page until you've established a personal page first. After all, it doesn't do much for your brand if you only have a couple of

Likes and no traffic. I didn't create a fan page until I had almost 1,900 friends on my personal page, but that was way too long to wait.

I recommend that you start your fan site when you have a good healthy following of at least three or four hundred on your personal site. On top of that, make sure that at least half of those are real fans and not friends or family. That way, when you start your fan site, it will be easier for the fans to transfer there and you'll have a modest following right from the start.

Facebook Promotion Overview

Using Facebook for promotion is a completely different animal than for casual personal use. Everything you post should have some thought put into it to get the best interaction. Let's look at how that's done.

What Should I Say?

A major concern that artists have is not only about what's appropriate to post, but also being afraid they don't have enough to say. Believe it or not, if you're popular enough to have fans, then you also have plenty to say that they'll be interested in. Things that you might consider mundane are anxiously scarfed up by super fans who crave every tiny tidbit. Here are some ideas to start with.

- **A behind the scenes story.** Fans love details, so don't be afraid to tell them where you're recording (don't give the exact name if you don't want to be disturbed) and why you chose the studio, location or rehearsal space. Other information that super fans want are things like how long it took to record or mix a song, when it was or will be released, and how the players, director, producer or engineer was hired.

- **Where the idea came from.** Every song came from somewhere and fans love to know when, where and how it was created. If you didn't write the song, you can still tell them what you did to bring the song to fruition during rehearsals, preproduction or recording. The same goes for the concept for a video.

- **The people involved, especially fans.** Who's the director, producer, engineer, musicians, cameraman, etc.? Was a fan involved in the selection or have anything to do with the project, gig, or tour?

TIP: Giving a shout-out to fans always takes precedence over anything else. It's the ultimate feel-good promotional tool.

- **Interviews with others on the project.** If you can't think of anything to say about the project, gig or tour, ask some of the others connected with it. Surely somebody has some unique insight that you just can't see.

- **Trivia about the project, no matter how small.** Real fans crave trivia. Things that you consider mundane and not worth mentioning could be a goldmine for a super fan. For instance, something as small as the fact that you keep breaking the G string on a certain guitar, which made you switch to a different heavier brand, seems like nothing to you, but some fan will find the fact totally fascinating. The same with the mic you used on the guitar amp or vocal when recording. How about the mic positioning? How about the kind of tea you drink before a gig to protect your voice?

Keep in mind that if you only have ten fans, there might only be one that finds the minutia compelling, but the super fans are the ones ultimately paying the bills and those are the ones to cater to.

TIP: Generally speaking, the things that people want to know are the things you take for granted.

Crafting A Promotional Post That Works

As stated a few times above, using Facebook for promotion dictates the way in which you post. That's because you have to craft each post in such a way that provides you with brand building, promotion and information. Let's look at some post examples.

"Having breakfast after the gig. Just had bacon, eggs and potatoes. The bacon was greasy and the potatoes were burnt. The coffee was good though."

This is a bad post and here's why. First of all it's way too personal. Who cares about your breakfast? Even if Beyonce or Adam Levine posted this it would still be boring. Second of all, it's too long. As you'll see, shorter posts tend to work better. About the only thing that's okay here is the fact that he mentioned it was after a gig, which provides a slight hint of something a fan might want to know, but where was the info about the gig?

Let's look at an improved example:

"Great gig at the Capitol tonite. You people ROK! 2 girls jumped on stage and Joey boogied with them."

This one's better because it gives us some information. The gig was at the Capitol (which we assume is a venue of some sort), then there's the shout-out to the fans that attended, which is always a good idea. Unfortunately, there's still something lacking. How about this one:

"Great gig at the Capitol tonite. You people ROK! 2 girls jumped on stage and Joey boogied with them. Pictures and video at http://theunsigned.com/pix."

This one's great because it gives us the same information, plus it gives us a link to actually see Joey boogying with the audience. The link is to the fictitious band (at least for this example) called "The Unsigned." Attach a picture to this and you have the best of all worlds.

Let's look at another example.

"Back in the studio today. Feeling tired after a long weekend of partying. Catching a cold."

Who cares that you're tired? And why should I feel sorry for you because you partied too hard? And your cold concerns us how?

This one's a bit better:

"In the studio today with Johnny Rox for some hi-energy rockabilly."

This post gives us some interesting info. We find out who he's in the studio with and the kind of music they'll be doing. It can still be improved though.

"Back in AIR studios today with Johnny Rox for some hi-energy rockabilly. Excellent rhythm section of Jack X and Ronaldo. Pictures at http://theunsigned.com/airpix."

This one almost has it all. It tells us where (AIR studios), with who (Johnny Rox) and even some of the details (the rhythm section of Jack X and Ronaldo). Then it tops it off with a link to some pictures. What would make this even better is if a picture were attached to the post.

Post Creation Rules

After seeing the comparisons between posts, you can see that we're observing a number of rules. They are:

1. Keep it short. Facebook suggests that somewhere between 100 and 250 characters (which equals a line or two of text) gets 60% more likes, comments and shares, while other studies have shown that posts of 80 characters or less get 23 percent more interaction. That said, don't restrict yourself if you can't tell the story or get the point across in a limited amount of characters.

2. Keep it professional. Just like when you're writing a press release, an article, or almost anything else, you want to keep to the basics of who, what, when, why and how. You don't have to get them all in there, but these are the things that make a post interesting. I'm a big believer that you should keep your personal feelings out of it as much as possible until you get a lot of experience posting, and even then have it only creep into the conversation occasionally. That way, you'll stay out of trouble with a post that might seem too controversial to some fans.

3. Include a link. Always include a link to additional information, pictures, video, mailing list, or your website. If you have someone's attention enough for them to read your post, it's likely they'll take action even further if given the chance.

That's said, the type of link that you include does make a difference. Using a long URL can get you three times the engagement on Facebook, mostly because people trust it more than one that's been shortened. What's the difference? Take a look:

Long URL:
http://bobbyowsinskiblog.com

Shortened URL:
bit.ly/vjgIUQ or ow.ly/eMLi2

Shortened URLs work great for Twitter when the number of available characters is limited, but always use the longer one for Facebook.

4. Include a photo. Posts with photos receive 39 percent more interaction than ones without. That said, posts with videos receive fewer likes and views, mostly because people don't want to commit the time it takes to watch an entire video. That's not to say that you should stay away from posting videos, just remember that in some cases, less is more. Native videos on Facebook are a different animal though, and we'll get into them more in a little bit.

5. Engage your fans. Ask them questions, ask their opinions, ask them anything, but get them talking to you and to your other fans. In social media, their participation really matters as it keeps the fan base healthy, and gives you feedback as to how you're doing and what they want from you. Posts with questions have 92% more comments, but be sure to place them at the end of the post.

6. Calls to action work. When fans are asked to Like a post, they do so at three times the rate than when they're not asked, as well as comment at a rate more than three times times the norm. When asked to share a post, they're seven times more likely to do so.

TIP: Be careful when using a call-to-action that asks for a Like, comment or share. This can violate Facebook's terms of service agreement and get you banned if you offer to trade something for it! There are ways to do this with a third party application (which we'll cover in a bit).

---

7. Bonus: Experiment with emoticons and emojis. What's the difference? An emoticon is a typographic display of a facial representation, used to convey emotion in a text only medium. Like so:

;-)

Emoji are actual pictures, of everything from a set of painted nails (🖐) to a slightly whimsical ghost (👻).

In some cases, emoticons and emojis can provide as much as 52% higher interaction, while in other cases, the interaction can be lower than average. Love and HaHa emojis have the highest interaction rates.

The Best Time To Post

While you might be writing the best, most engaging posts, they do you no good if there's no one reading. The question then becomes, "When is the best time of day to post on Facebook?"

The Studies

There have been many studies on the subject, but most of them have found pretty much the same thing:

- Facebook usage is highest at 11AM, 3PM, and 8PM ET.

- The biggest spike occurs at 3PM ET on weekdays.

- Wednesday at 3PM is the busiest Facebook period of the week.

- Fans are the least active on Sunday.

- Posts that occur in the morning tend to perform almost 40 percent better in terms of user engagement than those in the afternoon.

- The top of the hour (:00 to :15 minutes) sees more interaction than other parts of the hour.

- In what seems to be a contradiction, 65 percent of users only access Facebook when they're not at work or at school, which means in the evening.

- The highest clickthroughs come at 3PM ET on Wednesday, with links posted from 1PM to 4PM getting the highest average clickthroughs.

- Links after 8PM and before 8AM struggle for attention.

- Posts with questions have a 15 percent higher engagement rate. A question starting with the word "would" gets the most engagement, followed by "where," "when," and "should." "Why" gets the least engagement.

Like with many of the stats that we see online, you have to take some of these items with a grain of salt and see what works best for your specific application. The only thing that they all have in common is that posting at the top of the hour (i.e. 8AM) is a lot more effective than anything else.

In Practice

I have found that 8AM, 3PM and 8PM ET do indeed get the most traction, but 11AM can sometimes work as well. One of the things that I don't like about evening posts at 8PM ET is the fact that Facebook viewing begins to drastically drop off afterwards, meaning that the shelf life of the post is a lot shorter. That's why I personally try to make my final post of the day at 3PM at the latest.

TIP: *Release major stories in the early morning. If you post between 11AM to 4PM ET, you risk your content getting pushed down by News Feeds and other traffic.*

When it comes to the weekends, I've found that traffic definitely decreases. Since my Facebook posts are generally about my blog posts, I usually post a "week in review" post of only the blog post titles on

Saturday and Sunday. I've found that anytime in the morning generally works well, although I've settled on 9AM or 4PM ET most of the time.

I've also found that posts that contain a photo or graphic also do much better than those that don't have one. With so many posts being text only, one with any sort of graphic sticks out from the crowd. If the picture or graphic is in any way interesting or entertaining, all the better.

Scheduling Posts

After reading the last topic about timing your posts, you're probably thinking, "I just don't have the time to wait until exactly 3PM to post, and I'll be in a rehearsal at 8PM. How am I going to do this?" That's the beauty of the scheduling function within Facebook (see Figure 6.3). If you take notice there's a calendar icon on the bottom of the status update box where you post. You can schedule the post by clicking on the year, month, day and time.

Figure 6.3: Facebook scheduling

There's another way to schedule posts that may be a bit more streamlined, especially if you have more than one Facebook fan site and also post to other social sites like Twitter, Instagram and Google+. A number of services are available that not only help with scheduling, but with viewing posts and analytics as well. Although I happen to use Hootsuite (seen in Figure 6.4), there are a number of others that do basically the same thing. Here's a partial list, although new ones come available all the time.

- Hootsuite
- Tweetdeck
- Hubspot
- Buffer

- SocialFlow
- SproutSocial
- Spredfast

Figure 6.4: Scheduling posts with Hootsuite

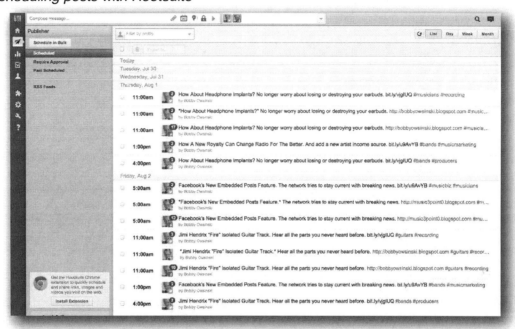

All of these services allow you to schedule your posts to at least Facebook and Twitter, and some post to other networks as well. Many have a free tier that's somewhat limited, and others will charge depending upon the features and analytics that you require.

One of the best parts about these services is that they also allow you to view all of your posts from the various networks and pages in one place, rather than continuously flipping through different social sites (see Figure 6.5). That allows you to view what's happening at a moments glance, a valuable time-saver when you have a lot of networks to tend to.

Post Frequency

Yes, it's true, you can post too much. Facebook suggests that one or two posts a day get the most response, and there's evidence that posting any more begins to become counterproductive. In fact, artists and bands that post more see 19% less interaction. Once again, less is more. It's better to have one great post than a number of mediocre ones.

How Facebook Determines What's In Your News Feed

One of the things that's most disturbing to users that regularly post on Facebook is how few of their posts their friends and followers actually see. At one point in time, 100% of all your followers would see every single thing that you posted. That figure went down to 15% a few years ago, and now stands at 2% or even less. That means that if you have 1,000 followers, on average only about 20 of them will see your post in their newsfeed unless you choose to pay to promote it.

What determines what the fan sees? Facebook uses a complicated algorithm called Edgerank that determines what posts to show your friends and followers that some insiders say covers thousands of factors. At it's most basic, the more popular the story, the more likely it will show up on a person's News Feed. What that means is that you have to optimize your content in order to make sure that it will have a high relevancy, and as a result be seen by more people. It's sort of like organic SEO, but just for Facebook.

In essence, what Edgerank does is personalize Facebook for each reader, so it's possible that many of your friends may not see every post that you make unless you keep things interesting. Just like with blogging, email newsletters, or any promotion online, you really have to work it to not only keep the audience that you have, but to grow it as well.

No one outside of Facebook knows exactly what the formula is, but it can be simplified into something like what you see here in Figure 6.6.

Figure 6.6: How Facebook determines what's in your newsfeed

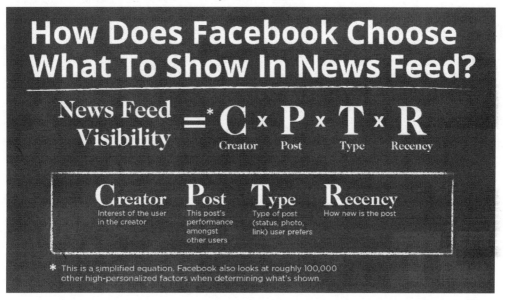

If formulas like this make your eyes glaze over, let's take a simpler look at how Facebook's algorithm chooses what appears and in what order. As said before, the algorithm is said to take into account thousands of different factors, but there are four main elements that decide a post's personalized relevancy score, and therefore its visibility to that user, as are illustrated in Figure 6.7.

Figure 6.7: How Facebook determines what's in your News Feed

1. Who Posted It – The more you've interacted with a post's author in the past, the more interested Facebook thinks you'll be in their future posts. This interaction could be engagement such as Liking or commenting, but also clicking or slowing down to read their posts, visiting their Page or profile, tagging them or being tagged together in posts or photos, and many other actions on Facebook. This is why you don't see posts from old friends or Pages you haven't interacted with in years.

2. How Other People Engaged With The Post – The more that other people have engaged with a particular post, the more likely that Facebook will show it to you too.

3. What Type Of Post It Is – The more that you typically engage with a certain kind of post like status, a link, a photo, a video, an event, a job change, or content from another app, the more Facebook will show you posts of that type. Different people enjoy different kinds of posts and Facebook matches people to post types. If you never watch videos, for instance, then you won't see many appear in your timeline.

4. When It Was Posted – The more recently a story was posted, the more likely you're going to see it. That said, Facebook also detects when you last checked your News Feed, and will automatically rank older posts higher if it knows you haven't logged in for a while and therefore haven't seen them. If you check your newsfeed a lot, then Facebook will prioritize very recent posts. If you're offline for a week then Facebook will show you an older post that it thinks you'll want to see even if it was posted a week ago.

There are other major factors the govern what you'll see as well.

5. How Many Others Have Posted the Same Thing – When lots of friends or Pages post or Like the same thing, Facebook assumes it's a big deal and will figure that you'll want to see it as well and pushes it up higher in the News Feed.

6. New Facebook Products – Facebook tends to favor new product releases and prioritizes them to test them out. That's why natively posted and live videos have a much greater reach than standard posts at the moment.

None of these factors mean much if you post boring or repeated content though, and in the end that's the key factor in gaining greater reach to your followers. If the people that see a post comment and share it with their friends, Facebook will take that into account immediately.

Improving Your Edgerank

In order to improve your Edgerank, and therefore how much you appear in your fans News Feeds, you must always be aware of the following (some of these we've covered already):

- **Post content that's relevant, engaging, and timely**.

- **Use photos and graphics where possible.** Photos are the most valuable and powerful content that you can post, followed by videos and then links.

- **Use time-based words** like "today," and if offering merch, "limited-time only."

- **Put your fans in charge occasionally.** Ask your fans questions. Let them decide which song will be the next single, or which video they like best, or the album cover artwork. They like to be involved and the news feed algorithm likes it as well.

- **Target your status updates.** If you have fans all over the world, most don't need to know about a local or regional gig or release. Target the appropriate posts as tightly as you can to the area necessary to get the word out (check out the post targeting example in Figure 6.8).

Figure 6.8: Facebook post targeting.

- **Diversify your content.** A combination of how-to's, artist or band trivia, breaking news, polls, fill-in-the-blanks, photos and videos, or third party content keeps it interesting.

The Facebook Like

One measure of how well you're doing on Facebook is the number of Likes that you receive either for your page or any particular post. The Like button allows a user to express his support or enjoyment for certain content. On Facebook, when a user clicks the Like button, the content then appears on his or her New Feed, so the content is then shared with his or her friends. The total number of Likes is also displayed.

Understanding The Like Button

It's important that you don't get too hung up on how many Likes you receive. People click the button because you've moved them enough that they want to endorse you or your post. That said, be careful how you assess a post that gets more Likes than you expect, since it may be that your fans are responding to a link, a photo, or even an emotion that was evoked, rather than to your cleverness.

Also remember that perhaps only two percent of your fans will see any given Facebook post, and only about one percent will Like it. For example, at the time this book was written, the Black Keys had about 4,000,000 fans and get around 2,000 to 4,000 Likes per post, as do Mumford and Sons with 5,000,000 fans. Every once in a while, a post might shoot to as many as 50,000, but most of the time the average still hangs around that 1% mark.

This applies to even major artists who may have millions of fans, but may see only dozens to 100's of Likes on some posts. For example, Figure 6.9 shows a post by Justin Bieber only received 1,600 Likes and only 28 comments, even though he has around 75 million followers. That's just 0.00002%!

Figure 6.9: Even celebs engagement can be low

By the time you read this, those follower numbers mentioned above will undoubtedly be higher, but the totals don't really matter. The point is that most posts receive far fewer than one percent Likes, and only the most popular ones come in at one percent or slightly above.

The reason why an artist should continue to post without worrying about getting Likes is the same reason why advertising works - *it's all about the impressions*. The more impressions, or views, the more likely the viewer will take some action at some point in time, like stream some of your music, go to a show, or buy a T-shirt.

That said, if you have 1,000 Facebook fans, this is what you can expect on an given post:

- Average post seen by 20 fans (2% of 1,000 fans)
- Average number of Likes = less than 10 (1% of 1,000 fans)
- Total impressions = 20 (the number of fans that see your post)

As long as the information you post is valuable to the reader in some way, it's worth doing because you're communicating and engaging. In other words, it's nice to be "Liked," but it's not necessarily a sign of a successful post.

TIP: Be careful not to be lulled into thinking that if someone doesn't register a Like or a Share, they're not actually reading the post. We all know that's not the case, because in fact many of us see and react to posts every day without actually registering a Like.

So Why Worry About Likes Anyway?

A Like is a form of social authority, but also don't forget that your #1 goal on Social Media (whether it's Facebook, Twitter, Google+, Pinterest, or Instagram) is to

Get People to Take Action.

In fact, Likes are actually one of the lowest forms of actions, with comments and shares meaning more in terms of engagement. That said, we want them anyway.

How To Get Facebook Likes

Likes aren't what they used to be in terms of the weight they carry. For one thing, it's now fairly easy to game the system by buying Likes (although that can be detected easily), but having them does carry some social authority. A page that has a lot of Likes makes you take notice, whether they've been bought or not.

But what we really want is organic Likes. How do we go about doing that? There are some common things to do first.

- **Include a photo.** Posts with photos get 53% more Likes, 104% more comments, and 84% more click-throughs.

- **Keep it short.** Posts with 80 characters or less get 66% more engagement.

- **Ask a question.** "Question" posts get 100% more comments.

- **Use fill-in-the-blanks posts.** Something like "I would be willing to _____ to go to the show."

- **Post at the right time.** Time of day and day of the week is important, as stated previously.

- **Include Facebook Like boxes on your website and blog.** Making your Facebook Page as discoverable as possible includes promoting your Facebook presence using the marketing channels you already have, and removing any barriers for existing contacts to like your page. If you have a website or blog, use Facebook's various social plugins to get people to 'Like' your page without having to go over to facebook.com.

- **Cross-promote on Twitter and Instagram.** Add a link to your Facebook Page on your Twitter and Instagram profiles (and your personal profile, for that matter). Tweet about your Facebook Page occasionally to encourage your Twitter followers and Instagram connections to stay in contact with you on another network.

- **You can also add your Twitter link to your Facebook Page, and occasionally tweet about your Facebook Page**. Don't stop with Twitter and Facebook; you could also cross-promote on LinkedIn, Flickr, YouTube, and any other platform that you're on. Just be sure that your cross-promotions are strategically placed so your other audiences won't feel like they're getting spammed.

- **Ask for a Like.** A few years ago, Facebook instituted a policy where you could get your account suspended for asking for a Like, comment or share. Today, it's still against its terms of service to ask for a share, but asking for a Like is now OK. It works if you ask nicely and don't ask too often.

Now let's look at some more advanced ways to increasing your Likes.

- **Run a timeline contest.** Once again, a few years ago you were forced to use an approved service outside of Facebook to run a contest, and while that may still be a good idea, today you can run a contest based on improving your Like total. Just make sure that you follow Facebook's rules or use a third party contest solution like votigo.com, gleam.io, shortstack.com or woobox.com.

- **Invite people who Like your post to Like your page.** Not many people know about this feature, as it only exists on fan and business pages (see Figure 6.10). When you click on the people who engaged with your post, you'll see three types of buttons:

    Invite – Clicking on this will invite the person who engaged with your post to Like your page.

    Liked – These are the people who have Liked your page already.

    Invited – These are the people who you have sent an invitation to, but haven't yet accepted.

Figure 6.10: Invite people who Like your page.

There is a limit to the number of invitations you can send per day, which seems to be somewhere between 500 and 1,000. Check back in a day or two to see if you can start inviting more people who have engaged with your posts. Don't expect all your invites to Like your page though. The average acceptance rate is between 15 and 20 percent.

• **Upload your audience.** Another way to get more likes is to upload you email list to Facebook, and those from that list who are on Facebook will be made more likely to see a suggestion to Like your page in places like "Suggest Page." Your contacts who aren't on Facebook won't see this suggestion.

To upload a list of email contacts through Facebook, click the ... selection below your pages cover photo, select "Suggest Page", and then select your mailing list provider and upload your contacts. Keep in mind that you can only upload a max of 7,000 per day and a max of 5,000 at any one time.

- Finally, if you have the budget for it, you can use some **paid advertising** to help augment the hard work you're already putting in. Facebook offers an easy way to set up an ad to promote your page. It contains a call-to-action suggesting that users Like your Facebook Page. These ads can appear in user's News Feeds or in the ad column on the right-hand side of their web browser when they're on Facebook.

We'll look more at Facebook advertising in an upcoming section.

TIP: *The words that lead to the most shares on Facebook are "best," "most," and those that explain, such as "why," and "how."*

The Land Of Fake Likes

It never takes long for someone to come up with a way to game an online measurement that the music industry finds useful. Once upon a time, the major labels used the number of MySpace followers as a measure of an artist's popularity. That was until it was discovered that there were multiple ways to fake those numbers and make them look larger than they actually were. Of course, the number of hits a website received were once used as a measurement too, until every unknown band seemed to have at least a million.

Now it's possible to purchase Likes as well, and the price goes anywhere from $0.01 to $1.07 for each one, depending upon the quantity purchased. The problem is that while having 10,000 Likes may look impressive, it's a foundation built on quicksand, since it gives you no indication of how well your real social media strategy is working. And as you can see from the Figure 6.11 below, it's pretty easy to spot if someone wants to take the time. Buying them really doesn't do anything except cost you money, so it's best to stay away.

Figure 6.11: Fake Likes that all originate in Mexico City

10 Best Facebook Posting Practices For Artists And Bands

Facebook is one of the best social networks for artists and bands, but execution is everything in order to take full advantage of it. Here are the 10 best practices for artists and bands to increase your engagement.

1. Reach out to other artists. Ask a band whom you're tight with to post your new music video/track/album art on their timeline with a link back to your Facebook Page, and then return the favor. This is one of the best ways to use the network to expand your audience.

2. Take your fans backstage. Everyone loves to see behind the scenes, but fans are especially interested. It might seem insignificant to you, but any kind of backstage access is a big deal to them.

3. Go beyond the music. Your music is your marketing, but don't forget to make any merch or touring info available as well. That said, don't try to sell to your fans, just make these things easily available if they want it.

4. Ask for input from fans. Communication is a two-way street and fans love to be asked their opinion on just about anything. Besides, they're your fans so they know what they want.

5. Be visual. Music is an aural medium for sure, but either still or moving pictures add so much to the entire package that you can't ignore them any more. Besides, it's so easy to take pictures these days or make short videos with your smartphone, so you can't use gear or expertise as excuses anymore.

6. Make everything an event. This is one of the secrets of multiple singles releases rather than full albums. Every release becomes an event. You can expand upon that idea in just about any direction, from gigs or giveaways on your birthday to your best fan's birthdays, to making every gig a special occasion. Use your imagination.

7. Don't just ask for things. Once again, communication is a two way street. You give some and you take some and vice versa. If you ask for information, give something away for free. This goes a long way in keeping your tribe happy.

8. Don't forget the basics. Bios, press kits, pictures, and logos are still important, so be sure to have links to where people can get them if they want.

9. Offer exclusive content. The way to a fan's heart is through exclusive content. If a fan can get exclusive mixes or videos that no one else can get, that legitimizes his or her fandom and makes them want it even more. Alternative mixes, outtakes, interviews are all inexpensive and easy to make content that any fan would love to have.

10. Use some tools. Make sure to take advantage of everything that Facebook has to offer, but also check out apps like Bandcamp or ReverbNation for their event, sales and music plugins as well. Those that use Facebook a lot don't often think about it, but there are a number of guidelines that you agreed to when you first created either your personal or fan page. These are worth being aware of since a violation is enough to get you banned from the service, which is something that you definitely don't want.

Facebook Video Basics

Facebook video is one of the hottest features on the platform. The company is in a war with YouTube for video supremacy and as a result, it pushes video content into the News Feed far more often than normal posts. That said, this applies only to native videos that are directly uploaded to Facebook, not videos that are embedded from YouTube or Vimeo via links or embed codes.

Facebook also claims that it's taken over the mantle of most watched from YouTube, but the difference in calculating what counts as a view between the platforms is really apples versus oranges. For Facebook, if you watch a video even with the sound off for just 3 seconds, it counts as view. On YouTube, the amount of time varies but you need far longer engagement before it's counted.

Facebook Rights Manager

One of the powers of YouTube is that it allows content creators to make money from the platform either by uploading original content, or more powerfully, by monetizing other users posted videos if they use your content. This is all based on the service's Content ID system that allows tracking of content so that the rights holder can choose whether to monetize it or not. Until recently, Facebook's major failing was that its Rights Manager didn't have a similar system in place, and as a result its usefulness was fairly limited. It was able to track when someone was using your content, but there were only two options: have the pirated content deleted, or leave it up for more reach and visibility but without getting paid for it.

Rights Manager has now added the ability to generate revenue from pirated video with a third monetization option that puts a mid-roll ad in the video. The revenue is then shared with the rights holder, who also gets to determine where in the video the 20 to 30 second ads will run (Facebook chairman Mark Zuckerburg has mandated that the standard pre-roll commercials that you see on most YouTube monetized videos will not happen on Facebook videos and it will use mid-roll ads that will appear sometime after the 30 second mark instead).

Like YouTube, Facebook is paying 55% of the ad revenue to the rights holder. This split has been a bone of contention with the music industry, and it's not too happy with the fact that Facebook is matching YouTube's split rather than paying something closer to the industry standard 70% plus that streaming services pay. That said, now you can at least be paid something for views that not that long ago would pay nothing.

The problem is that Rights Manager is not something that automatically comes with having a Facebook account. You have to apply for it first, which can be done at rightsmanager.fb.com.

While the revenue division isn't making the music industry jump for joy, the fact that any new revenue stream for artists is a good one. Not only that, Facebook seems to be gaining both strength and users while YouTube's interest is waning a bit. Streaming has taken its toll on YouTube as a music source, but those same people that are now Spotify and Apple Music customers still remain on Facebook.

Designing A Video For Facebook

While you're probably going to upload a video that you've already posted on YouTube, there are some things to keep in mind when posting it to Facebook. In some cases, it might be better to customize the video a bit in order to get more engagement, since it's more of a social platform. Here's how to optimize your videos just for Facebook.

1. Limit the length to 5 minutes or less (way less). The shorter the video, the more plays you'll get (this applies for any platform). A long video can scare off people who might ordinarily check it out. That said, Facebook is transitioning to longer videos, especially if advertising is involved, so make sure that it's at least a minute long.

2. Create a good thumbnail image for your video. A good thumbnail is like a good cover of a book. It helps get an impulse "buy."

3. Create a catchy or unique title. Just like with a book or magazine article, the title can sell the product. Of course, this is just the same on YouTube as well.

4. Check out the keywords for similar videos. For example, if your song has a drum solo, you might want to check out what keywords other videos of songs with drum solos use as well.

5. Allow people to share your work. This sounds like a no-brainer, but many artists actually limit the sharing of their videos. Let your fans embed your video on their blogs and websites if they want. That's how you go viral and make money if you choose to monetize them.

6. Encourage people to rate and review your video. Ask for a Like, comments or a rating. Don't ask viewers to tag it or share it, however, since that's against Facebook's terms of service.

7 Tips For Publishing Facebook Videos

Creating a video is one thing, but publishing it is another. Here are some things you can do to get more engagement from your videos.

1. Schedule your videos for the time that the most fans will see it so the content stays fresh. The best time is between noon and 3PM (see Figure 6.12).

Figure 6.12: Scheduling Facebook video posts

2. Set an expiration date to help with any licensing restrictions. If you're posting something that might have a copyright problem, this is one way to get around it (see Figure 6.13).

Figure 6.13: Setting up a post expiration date

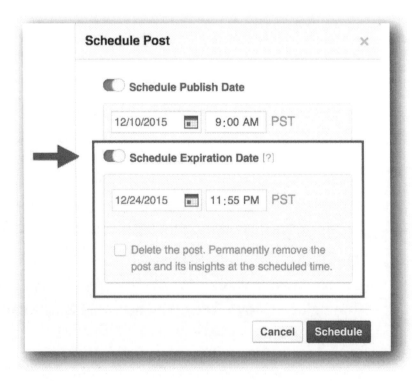

3. Add captions to tell your story without sound, since many viewers watch the video with the audio turned off (see Figure 6.14).

Figure 6.14: Adding captions

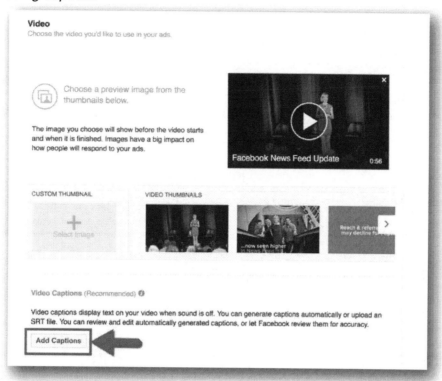

4. Edit and manage your videos with Facebook's video library tools (see Figure 6.15).

Figure 6.15: Accessing the editing tools

5. Take advantage of Facebook's embedded video player to be able to embed them on other platforms (see Figure 6.16).

Figure 6.16: Embed code for the video player

6. Utilize secret videos that must be accessed through a dedicated URL so they're only available to fans (see Figure 6.17).

Figure 6.17: Setting up a secret video

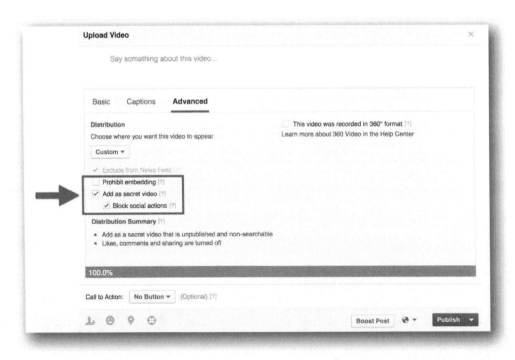

7. Track your metrics, especially your top videos, engagement and retention graphs (see Figure 6.18).

Figure 6.18: Live video analytics

Facebook videos allow you to reach more of your audience without having to pay for the privilege than with normal posts, so they're a powerful way for extending your brand and growing your audience.

Using Facebook Live

What is Facebook Live? Live lets artists, musicians, bands and producers share live video with their followers and friends on Facebook.

Facebook Live is another more recent release on the platform, and it seems like it will be a boon for artists and bands wanting to engage with their fans on the service. Facebook likes to promote fresh content, so Live videos are more likely to appear higher in News Feeds when those videos are actually being recorded live, than when they're watched later after the live recording.

Live is available to all Pages and profiles on Facebook for iOS, Android, and Facebook Mentions. When creating a Live video, keep the following in mind:

- The video will be published to your Page or profile so that fans and friends who missed it can watch it at a later time. You can remove the video post at any time, just like any other Facebook post.

- Videos will appear in the News Feed and on the your Page or profile while they are live. Once a broadcast has ended, live videos are eligible to show up everywhere that other videos appear.

- Live broadcasts can last up to 90 minutes, and even though Facebook encourages longer videos, shorter is still better, especially when it comes to replays.

TIP: Remember that you need a strong Internet signal before going live. WiFi tends to work best, but if you can't find a nearby network, you'll want at least a 4G connection. To check your internet speed ahead of time, download the Speedtest app from the App Store or Google Play.

Facebook encourages users to create videos that are more than five minutes long, with the logic being that the longer a clip is, the more time people will have to find it while it's still happening. Remember that Facebook's News Feed takes a while to update, so it needs some time to alert users that the video is occurring.

Facebook Live is great for boosting the numbers of people watching and engaging with live video and the company has touted the fact that comments are eight times more frequent on live than regular video. Generally speaking, it's a pretty horrible experience when rewatching though, so expect the best to happen during the initial broadcast.

Seven Ways To Increase Your Facebook Fan Engagement

Fan engagement is the best way to increase your Facebook fan base. Here are six ways for that to happen that you should always keep in mind.

1. Engage, but don't advertise. The soft sell always works best. The key to Facebook is all about engagement and the best way for that to happen is to get rid of the "Listen To My New Album" thinking. Instead, try asking a question like:

"Hey everyone, we just released our new album. We're trying to decide on the next single. Please have a listen and leave a comment about your favorite tracks. [link to your album on your store site]"

2. Ask questions, or **ask for your fan's support.** This is one of the best ways to engage them without hard-selling them. Remember that when fans leave a comment or review, it will appear on their friend's News Feeds, and other people are much more likely to check you out after online recommendations from friends.

3. Give a virtual high-five. It's important to respond to any comment that's posted. At the very least, "Like" their comment. This is the online equivalent of a high-five from the stage. A Like, a response, a thank you, or a shout out is a subtle way to reward your fans. When they see a status update from you, they'll be thrilled, and they may even share it again.

4. Reward fans, then ask them to reward their friends. Exclusive tracks or videos are a great way to reward your fans. The idea is to either capture the fan's information or get them to share it with their friends, which increases your reach by hitting their friend's feeds. Once you capture the fan's info, you can then build the relationship. Many times, they'll later reciprocate with a purchase of merch or by attending a live show.

5. Advertise yourself to fans of similar artists. Facebook makes it incredibly easy and affordable to create an ad that's perfectly targeted to your demographic (see the section on Facebook ads coming up).

6. Make everything an event. This is one of the secrets of multiple single song releases rather than full albums. Every release becomes an event. You can expand upon that idea in just about any direction, from gigs or giveaways on your birthday to your best fan's birthdays, to making every gig a special occasion.

7. Always be ready to sell. The best time to get the fan to act is when the fan is excited, and that's when they discover your music. Your chances of making a merch or ticket sale are greater if they can purchase directly on Facebook instead of somewhere else.

These ideas are something that you should consider, since Facebook is one of the most powerful social media tools at your disposal.

Promoting Posts

Another thing that Facebook allows you to do is to pay to promote individual posts. Regular unpromoted posts are typically seen by only 2 to 3 percent of your friends, but choosing to promote a post will include a larger portion of your friends and make the post appear higher in their News Feeds.

You can only choose to promote a post on your fan page, and this can be done by clicking on the *Boost* button located at the bottom right of a post. You'll now be taken to a pay screen where you'll be asked to enter your credit card number or select Paypal. The cost must be at least $2 (although you can select any price higher than that as well), and the post will now be marked "Sponsored." Then select your audience and duration that you want to post to be promoted. You'll be able to check to see how many more people saw it as a result of the paid promotion once the boosted post begins.

Is promoting a post worth it? Record labels and marketers for big brands alike claim that it can be very effective if your target audience is selected carefully. The best thing is to dive in and give it a try a few times while keeping your allocated money on the low side. If you have a post that you feel strongly about, has a call to action and a link to where you want the audience to go, it's worth a shot.

TIP: *Only choose to promote a post if you think that the post will still be relevant for at least three days after the promotion begins.*

6. Name, price and schedule. This is the area where you name your campaign, select the amount of money you want to spend, and schedule it (see Figure 6.21). The beauty of Facebook ads are that you get to choose the price you want to pay, and how often you want to pay. If you only have $5 to spend a week, you can schedule the ad to run continuously until that amount is reached, schedule that amount per day, or even choose to run on a day in the future.

You can also choose whether you want to pay for impressions or clicks. An ad based on the number of people that see the ad means that you're paying for impressions, measure in CPM, or cost per thousand. If you want to pay for only the people who click through to your site, that's pay-per-click. One of the problems with this is that you may pay for clicks that don't turn into actions, which can eat up your budget fast. That's why it's best to only choose this option after you've had some experience using the CPM model first.

TIP: Your bid amount is based upon how precise your target audience is. Adjust your target audience to receive a more favorable bid price.

An Overview Of The Ad Manager

The next step up from promoting your posts is placing ads on Facebook and that's done with part of the platform know as the Ad Manager. There are some pretty intense courses centered around Facebook advertising as it can be a pretty deep subject, so we'll only scratch the surface here. This should be enough to get you placing your own ads though, or even promoting your posts with much more precise targeting than from boosting them.

All ads are part of a campaign. A campaign can have multiple ad sets, and each ad set can have many different ads. For instance, in a campaign you might want to have a different ad set for the US, Canada, and the UK, and slightly different ads, target audiences and budgets for each country (see Figure 6.19). Each ad set might have several different variations of the same ad, with perhaps a different headline or target, that you'll test to find the one that works the best.

Figure 6.19: An typical ad campaign

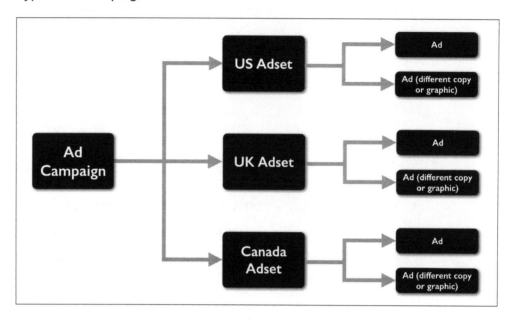

Before you begin, be sure to clearly define your objectives and goals. Do you want more post or page Likes? Do you want to expose more people to your music or videos? Do you want to sell more merch? Do you want more website or blog traffic? Make sure you understand what your priorities are before launching into an ad campaign, since the more uncertain you are, the less likely your campaign will succeed.

After you've figured that out, go to the Create Ads link under the downward arrow on the top right side of your Facebook page and you're off.

TIP: You can only create an ad from your administration page, which means your personal page.

Placing Your Ad

Designing and placing your ad is pretty simple, thanks to the advert layout page of the Ad Manager.

1. First, select your goal. The first page will ask you to name your campaign and select your marketing objective. You're given 10 goal choices broken into three categories to choose from, as seen in Figure 6.20.

Figure 6.20: Selecting the promotion goal

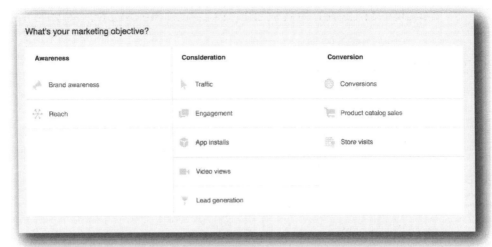

The objectives most appropriate for when you're just starting are Traffic, Engagement, Video Views or Lead Generation.

- **Traffic** will send people to a destination on Facebook, like your page, or completely off Facebook, like to your website.

- If you want more page Likes, post engagement, or event responses, then **Engagement** is the one to choose.

- **Video views** is pretty self-explanatory, while **Lead Generation** is designed to collect email addresses from people that are interested in your brand or music without them having to leave Facebook for an external landing page.

2. Next you'll be asked to target your audience. One of the best things about Facebook ads is that you're able to precisely target your audience. You can target the location either on a country, state, city or zip code level, as well as age, gender, interests, relationship status and even friends of connections, and more.

To reach the right people, type in names of similar artists in the "Precise Interests" field. That will target your ad to people who entered that artist as music they listen to. Also, pick a geographic region that makes sense. If you're a touring artist or band, you might want to only select the areas where you'll be performing to target people to come to your shows.

You'll also be asked if you want your ads automatically placed in Facebook's various distribution points (News Feed, Instant Articles, In-Stream Videos, Right Column, Instagram Feed or Stores, Audience Network) or if you want to do it manually. Until you get more experience with Facebook ads, select *Automatic Placements*.

TIP: To reach the right target, type in names of similar artists in the "Precise Interests" field. That will target your ad to people who like that artist. Also, pick a geographic region where you're active.

3. Next you're asked to select a budget and schedule. You can set this up on a daily basis, or for the lifetime of the campaign. This can be as little as $1 per day, depending on the type of ad you're creating, but usually $5 is the least you want to do in order to get any meaningful response. You'll then be asked to schedule you ad. I recommend that you select "Set a start and end date" and fill in the exact dates you want your ad to begin and end. You can always change this as you go, as it's easy to adjust the budget or the end date at any time in the future as the campaign is running.

4. Next is Optimization for Ad Delivery. Select an Automatic Bid Amount until you get more experience with Facebook ads. Even with a lot of experience, this is usually the best selection.

5. Now it's time to create your ad. First select the format. It can be a single image, a single video, a carousel (which is an ad with two or more scrollable images or videos), a slideshow with a loop of up to 10 images, or a canvas that has a combination of graphics and videos. Keep it simple at first and just select the single image or video until you get more experience.

6. Next you need to locate the image that you'll be using. It can come from your library of uploaded images to Facebook, from some free stock images, or you can upload a new one from your computer. Take notice on the right the Ad Manager provides the recommended image size and ratio.

TIP: Be especially careful of any graphic with text in it. The text can take up no more than 20% of the picture or less, or you ad may be rejected.

7. Connect to your Facebook page. If you have multiple fan pages, this is where you select it. If you have a particular post that you want to promote, this is where you'll select it as well.

8. Select your destination URL. This is the URL that people will be sent to when they click on your ad.

9. Now add a brief headline, then some text that explains what you're advertising. You can now select from a number of calls to action.

10. Finally review your ad before you confirm you want to run it, then select *Place Your Order*. Your ad will be checked by Facebook before it goes live, so you'll see a *Pending* designation when you're sent back to the main page of the Ads Manager. Ads are approved or rejected usually within a couple of hours, but 24 hours at most.

TIP: *Fine tune your ad as you go along. Set it up, check back to see how well it's working, then change your settings to see if you can increase your reach.*

In general, it's been found that Facebook ads definitely do drive behavior on Facebook and even big brands like Ford, Subway, Dr. Pepper, Tide, among others find them effective. Page ads are a great way to build Likes, while post ads drive engagement and build your audience. Plus, you don't have to spend a lot of money to do it. It's a great option without having to worry about breaking the bank.

Keep in mind that Facebook advertising is a much more in-depth subject than has been presented here. One of its better features is called the Power Editor, which allows you to quickly duplicate ads so you can run split ad tests with different headlines, pictures, and targeting, but its use is somewhat more complex and goes beyond the scope of this book.

Try the simple Facebook ads as presented in this section first, get a feel for how everything works, then progress on to the other features of the Ad Manager or Power Editor after you've had some experience.

TIP: *A tracking pixel is a piece of invisible code that you insert on your webpage that allows Facebook to measure if an action was taken or not. This insures that you can measure the engagement on sites outside of Facebook.*

Facebook Policies Everyone Should Know

Those that use Facebook a lot don't often think about it, but there are a number of terms that you agreed to when you first created both your personal and fan page. These are worth being aware of since a violation is enough to get you banned from the service, which is something you definitely don't want to happen.

For example, Facebook has a number of guidelines for your cover graphic like:

- It can't have price or purchase information in the photo (like "50% off").

- It can't include a call to action to Like, comment or share with your friends.

- It can't include contact info like web, email or mailing address (there are better places to put this rather than on the cover photo as well).

When it comes to advertising, Facebook can be really picky not only with your ad, but the post-click experience as well. For instance:

- **The ad can't make any unsubstantiated or sensational claims.** While this is aimed more at the get-rich schemes that promise "Make a million dollars in less than a month," it can also be something as simple as "This is the best music experience you will ever have."

- **The ad must accurately reflect the product being sold on the landing page.** If you have a picture of a pretty girl, but a click takes the fan to a page that tries to sell him your latest vinyl album, that's a violation. If you're selling a piece of merch like a coffee cup looks like it's made out of solid gold but it's really made out of plastic, that's a violation.

- **When someone clicks on your ad, the landing page must convey clear info about the product.** Is the landing page misleading in any way? If instead of an album, it looks like the viewer is getting a trip to a tropical island, that's a violation.

- **You cannot have exit popups.** Everyone hates popups, but the fact is, they really work. That said, if someone visits your landing page through a Facebook ad but encounters a popup if she tries to exit the page, that's a violation.

- **You can't offer a discount that's more than 50% off.** Facebook thinks that more than a 50% discount is excessive.

- **You can't have a fake countdown timer or fake limited inventory counter.** These are common tactics to compel someone to purchase, but to Facebook, they're a violation.

- **You cannot pretend to be an independent media entity of you're not.** You probably won't do this, but you can't place an ad that looks like it's from Rolling Stone magazine if that's not the case.

- **If you ask for a piece of personal info (like an email address, name, phone number, or address) in conjunction with a sale, you must state the price, billing interval, how to cancel, plus have an opt-in checkbox for the terms and conditions.** The checkbox can't be opted-in by default, and the information can't intentionally be hidden.

Other Best Practices

- Your landing page for a product you're selling should include links back to Facebook.

- You should have both a "Contact Us" and "About Us" tab on your landing page.

- Finally, one of the biggest violations of Facebook's terms of service agreement is that you can't promise to give someone something if they Like, comment or share your post unless you use a third party app.

Believe it or not, there are even more guidelines that what's in this section. To see all of Facebook's ad policies, go to facebook.com/policies/ads/

Marketing With Twitter

Twitter is great for building your brand and an amazing way to reach a lot of people that you probably couldn't reach any other way. That's said, after eleven years and over 300 million daily active users, many musicians are still confused by Twitter. Many seem baffled as to why anyone would want to use a service providing short 140 character messages, or why they should be bothered using it as a promotional tool. Top that off with the many horror stories of PR disasters started by the errant tweet from celebrities and professional athletes, and they're skittish about even getting involved in this highly successful social network.

The flaw in that thinking is that Twitter works and works well for promotion and marketing, if you know how to do it. That's what this chapter is all about.

Twitter Basics

Twitter is a social platform that allows you to communicate with others in short, 140 character (or fewer if you want) messages called "tweets." You can think of it as a broadcast service, where your tweet is available for the world to see, but the ones that directly see it are your "followers," (sometimes called "tweeps," which is short for Twitter + peeps) which are people who've decided they like what you have to say. Whenever you tweet, your followers will be see your tweet in a timeline on their Twitter page. You can also tweet directly to a person who is following you, which is called a Direct Message or DM. If you like a tweet that you see, you can spread the word to your followers by Retweeting, or RT.

Twitter allows you to "favorite" a tweet, which is sort of like a bookmark. If there's something that you like or find useful, by favoriting a tweet you create a list that everyone can see on your profile.

When you sign up for a Twitter account (it's free) you get to select your screen name. This usually comes after the @ sign, so as an example my Twitter name is @bobbyowsinski. When you see a tweet that starts with someone's screen name, that means there's a public conversation going on with that person.

TIP: Give plenty of thought to your screen name. Be sure that it's as short as possible yet stays consistent with your website, Facebook, and other social sites.

While we're not going to tackle the basics of using Twitter, one recent feature that you should be aware with is that media attachments and quotes from other tweets are no longer considered part of the 140 character limit. That gives you a lot more room to make your thoughts be known.

Following And Followers

When you like what someone's tweeting and want to view all of their tweets, you follow them. Like Facebook, you can organize the people that you're following into lists so that it's easier to keep track of the information you want. These lists can be public or private. If you decide you don't like what someone is tweeting, or the volume of tweets is too heavy, you can simply unfollow them.

TIP: When you first sign up, Twitter will help you go through your address book to see if anyone you know is a Twitter user already. You then have the option to invite them to follow you.

When people follow you, it's an unwritten rule that you should follow them back, although I don't believe that's absolutely necessary. One way that many people are taught to get a lot of followers quickly is to follow everyone that they can find, hoping that they'll reciprocate. That works, but it's an empty gesture, as you want real followers that are truly interested in what you have to say. If you want to use that approach, try to stay at least within your genre of music and with people that have common interests.

That said, if you follow some of my upcoming advice, you'll get plenty of followers organically, but only if you're really are worth following in the first place.

Twitter Etiquette

This is a fairly simple medium, but there are certain unwritten rules that attempt to keep people from annoying one another. Despite this group etiquette, you'll still no doubt run into situations that may make you want to scream, but keep in mind that it's probably bugging others as well. Rest assured that sooner or later the offender gets the message and either mends his ways or leaves. Let's take a look at what you should know.

- **Don't use all caps.** One of the things that people online universally hate is someone COMMUNICATING IN ALL CAPS. This is considered the equivalent of shouting, is more difficult to read, and just plain impolite.

- **Don't be rude.** What's rude in real life is rude on Twitter as well. The problem is that people are more easily offended online because they can't see any facial expressions or body language, and as a result, what you consider to be a rather harmless tweet can kick up a firestorm. The way around this is to think through every tweet before you send it and stay away from any provocative language.

- **Don't use an affiliate link in a tweet.** Links in a tweet are a good thing, but it's bad form to include one that's blatantly trying to sell something or make money.

- **Don't ask someone for a favor publicly.** Just like doing it in a crowded room, it's uncool. Better to ask in a private conversation. Use DM instead.

- **Don't auto-DM.** It's possible to set up an automatic direct message welcoming someone when they follow you. Save your time and money as this is considered bad form. If it's not personal, an auto-DM can do more harm than good.

- **Issue a high volume warning.** If you're going to be tweeting more than normal (like from a show, conference or event), tell your followers in advance. No one likes their Twitter feed to be controlled by one person.

- **Don't be negative.** Nothing turns off followers faster than negative commentary. If you can't say something nice and be positive, don't say it at all.

- **Don't provide too much information.** Twitter isn't a place for details. There's not enough room in the limited number of characters that you have, which means that you have to resort to more tweets, which puts you into the realm of over-tweeting. As with most things online, less is more.

- **Pause between tweets.** Another thing that makes people crazy is a big volley of tweets one after the other. Take a break before your next tweet. Give other people a chance to get their tweets seen as well.

Following these online etiquette rules will not only help you keep your followers, but will keep you in good Twitter standing. It's just a little bit of courtesy, but well worth it.

Your Twitter Profile

Many artists, bands, brands and companies sign up for a Twitter account but don't take the time to properly create a profile. This is important because you'd be surprised at the number of times that people who are interested in you want more details about who you are. They get that info first from your profile, which can be linked to your website or Facebook page. Here's how to get the most from your profile.

- **Upload a photo.** Just like Facebook, a profile picture is important because it gives people confidence in you, your band or your product. Instead of a picture, this could be a logo as well. Resist the temptation to post a baby picture or avatar, or worse yet, nothing.Remember that all profile pictures should be 400 x 400 pixels.

- **Your bio.** You get all of 160 characters to provide your story. This allows you to get right to the essence of what it is that you do. You can also place a link here, although there's a place for a link to your website that's not part of the 160 characters.

- **The header.** It's now possible to upload a photo or graphic for the background of your bio, called the header. It's recommended that this graphic be 1500 x 421 pixels, but anything close to that size with a 3 to 1 length to width ratio will work. You can also resize the picture or have it automatically resized for you.

That's all it takes for creating a profile that looks consistent with your online look, and provides the right look and information when someone clicks on it.

Using Twitter For Promotion

As with Facebook, just being on Twitter isn't enough; you have to use it properly for it to be successful as a marketing tool. That means it's not just the fact that you tweet, but how and why you do it. Let's take a look.

What Should I Say?

Once again we come to the dilemma of what's worthy of posting, or in this case, tweeting. Here's a quick list:

- announcements
- events
- upcoming gigs
- post-gig comments
- backstage comments
- blog posts
- new song or video releases

- contests
- questions
- fan shout-outs
- current industry news or your views on it
- artist or band trivia

These are just a few ideas about what to tweet about. One of the reasons why tweeting from events works well is because Twitter is all about the latest news, and tweeting from an event is about has fresh as you can get. You also receive the added byproduct of being perceived as an expert as well.

Crafting A Promotional Tweet That Works

As with Facebook, it's how you say it as much as what you say that makes a difference. Let's look at a typical post from the band we're following in this book - The Unsigned.

Rehearsal soon. Need to go to the store to get something to drink. Bottled water is so expensive these days so I'll take Gatorade.

This is only 130 characters long, but just like some of our previous Facebook post examples, it doesn't tell us much that we care about hearing. It's an endorsement for Gatorade perhaps, but that doesn't help your marketing very much. How about this one instead:

At rehearsal in The Cave. Working on two new songs for the next Unsigned record. Producer Joey M with us. bit.ly/U3bbYA

Here we have a nice concise 119 characters that tell us a lot. We find out that the band (The Unsigned) is rehearsing at a place called The Cave (the fans my already know what and where that is), that they're working on new songs for an upcoming recording, and that their producer is in attendance. Plus, they've included a link so that you can see either some photos or a video. It's the perfect who, what, when, and why post, complete with a link for more information.

Personally, I always tweet the title of my latest blog post along with a short description and a link like this:

Making Money From YouTube. A new strategy for using YouTube views as a revenue source. bit.ly/u9AvYB #musicmarketing #musicians

This works because of the information that it provides, which is the promise to more info if you follow the link. We have the name of the post, a short description, the link, and then a couple of words preceded by a #, called a "hashtag." That's what we'll cover next.

TIP: Even though each tweet has a maximum of 140 characters, studies have found that tweets are more effective if they're less than 120.

The Hashtag: The Secret Behind Successful Tweets

Hashtags are simply keywords with the pound sign (#) in front of them. It's an unofficial feature of Twitter that's now widely accepted and supported, and is an easy way for people to search for and find a particular topic. It's also the best way to build your Twitter following.

Here's how it works, using one of my own tweets.

The Secret To The Merch Table. Want to sell more merch at gigs? Here's how. bit.ly/7GFjDq #merch #bands

This is a simple tweet regarding a post from my Music 3.0 blog a while back, complete with a shortened URL link. At the end are the hashtags #merch and #bands. That means that anyone who does a Twitter search for those keywords will see my post and follow me if they're so inclined.

Here's another way I could've used the hashtags in this tweet.

The Secret To The #Merch Table. Want to sell more merch at #gigs? Here's how. bit.ly/7GFjDq

In this case I embedded the hashtag directly into the tweet text. This works too but I find it too difficult to read, which can quickly turn into a negative for less sophisticated users that think they're looking at some sort of code they don't understand. Leaving some room at the end for the tags works a lot better, although it does consume more characters.

Here's another example.

Mix Comparison: From Rehearsal To Master. A mix at various stages of production. bit.ly/vjgIUQ #musicians #recording #bands

In this case there are three hashtags at the end, which really isn't a good practice. It's been found that more than two hashtags can actually be counterproductive.

Selecting Hashtags

Now that you know what a hashtag is, you're probably wondering how to select them. Here's how to do it.

Looking back to the first tweet above where both "merch" and "bands" appear in the tweet:

1. I researched the potential keywords first to see what kind of activity each word had by going to hashtagify.me, and selecting "Table Mode."

2. On the site I did a search for "#merch" and determined that there was a sizable enough result that it was worth using (see Figure 7.1). If the search hadn't turned up any results, I would have tried a different word instead. Since it came up with a popularity score over 44%, I knew that the hashtag was something that was searched for often, reached my target audience, and was therefore a good candidate to use in the tweet.

Figure 7.1: Search for #merch on hashtagify.me.

All-time Top 10 Hashtags related to #merch

Save as Bundle Copy Compare   Filter:

Hashtag	Popularity	Correlation	Weekly Trend	Monthly Trend
#merch	50.2	100%	-5.6 ▼	-4.2
#streaming	67.0	5.7%	+0.2	-0.5
#music	87.7	3.5%	-0.4	-1.5
#brand	68.4	3.3%	-1.2	-1.5
#fashion	84.3	3.2%	0.0	-3.3
#tshirt	66.5	3.0%	-1.0	-2.3
#mobile	76.3	2.9%	-0.2	-2.6
#LinkedIn	67.4	2.9%	-1.2	-3.4
#events	66.2	2.9%	-0.6	-2.5
#TouchpointEntertainment	28.6	2.9%	0.0	0.0
#in	72.5	2.9%	+0.5	-3.7

3. One of the other things that comes from a hashtag search is ideas for other hashtags. In this case a number of candidates came up when I tried an alternate - "#merchandise," which brought up alternatives like #promotional, #apparel, #tshirts, #clothing and #fashion.

TIP: Keep a list of potential hashtag candidates. You'll always find a place where some will be more appropriate than others.

I did the same thing to find the hashtags for the second tweet. I did a quick search and discovered that #mixing had more results than #mixer (there was also some confusion with a food processor as well), so that's the one I chose.

Hashtag Sites

There are a number of sites where you can do searches to come up with the appropriate hashtags.

- **hashtagify.me** is an all-purpose hashtag search site. You can find hashtags related to the hashtag you selected, trending hashtags, the most 30 most popular hashtags related to your search, and the popularity of related hashtags. There are several ways to look at your search results, from either ballon or table modes, as well as top influencers and usage patterns. If you select "In-depth Intelligence," you can purchase a number of premium programs to make your search even more granular.

- **hashtags.org** has gone through a number of changes over the years. It gave you straight up hashtag info at first, then disappeared for a while, and now provides trending information that gets more granular for a price. It's still worth checking out since you can get a larger picture of how a particular hashtag is being used.

Remember that a quick look at both the searches and trends before you select a keyword can make a difference in your Twitter traffic, which ultimately attracts new followers.

Rules For Using Hashtags

To get the most out of your hashtags, remember these rules:

1. Capital letters don't matter, but they do make it more readable.

2. Plurals matter. For instance, there's a big difference between #app and #apps.

3. Spaces and hyphens can't be used.

4. Don't use special characters or a hashtag with only numbers, and don't start one with numbers.

5. Don't use more than two per post.

Other Uses For Hashtags

While you're probably mostly concerned about building your brand by tweeting using hashtags, they do have other uses that are more widely used. Here are a few:

- **Breaking News.** Because Twitter is mostly a broadcast medium, it's excellent for breaking news. As an example, if you can't drive down the street because of a traffic jam, a quick look on Twitter will probably tell you the reason long before you'll hear it on the news. In fact, one of the reasons that the Arab Spring in 2010 was so successful was because of quick information exchanges through Twitter using hashtags like #LibyaFeb17 and #arabspring.

  Want to know what's happening in a town you're going to? Do a search for #Cleveland (or whatever town) and you'll know in a flash. Want to know the most up to date news on an event, just do a hashtag search for the event and you'll know more than most journalists covering the story. Twitter means instant news, and you can use that to your benefit.

- **Branding**. Movies and television shows now use hashtags as a way of promoting the show and as a gateway to second screen activity. Generally you'll see the # with the name of the movie or show behind it. Of course, this can be used for artists and bands as well. In the case of our fictitious band The Unsigned it might be #Unsigned or #TheUnsigned.

- **Complaints**. Hashtags have become a major way for Twitter users to express their displeasure with something, be it a product or service. This is sometimes known as a "bashtag." An example of this is when McDonalds customers shared their discontent by using the hashtag #McDhorrorStories, which was latter shortened to just #McDstories.

  Sometimes a person can show anger at a situation with something like #HateBadService or #AnnoyingWaiters, but these do nothing more than let off some steam unless they begin to be widely used.

- **Comments**. The opposite of a bashtag is a positive comment like #BeautifulDay or #GreatMusic. Once again, these serve no purpose other than to make a point, since they generally don't focus on a specific situation or event.

TIP: *Stay away from bashtags or anything negative as this can grow out of proportion quickly to the point where you won't be able to control the story. Negative usually begets negative.*

Remember that using hashtags is a great way to help people find you, but *don't forget to include a link* in your tweet to take them to your blog or website as well, since that's the real goal.

Tweet Frequency

Tweets don't live very long. Although the lifetime of a tweet is two hours at most, 92 percent of all retweets and 97 percent of all replies happen within that critical first hour. After that, they're as good as gone. That's why you may want to repost a tweet a second time if it's an important announcement. You'll probably have a completely different audience in the morning than later in day, so this is a strategy that can work without disturbing your followers too much.

What I usually do is post a tweet in the morning and repeat it later in the day, only with a different set of hashtags. That way, a tweet can have twice the potential reach to new followers. I also make sure that there's at least four hours between repeated tweets.

The Best Time To Tweet

If you're using social media for promotion, then you already know that the timing of when you post is critical to your success. Do it when most people are busy and not paying attention and you'll never get your message in front of them.

Chapter 6 illustrated that the ideal times for Facebook posts were at 11AM, 3PM and 8PM Eastern time. Studies also show that later in the day is the best time to tweet as well.

According to Dan Zarrella, a researcher at Hubspot who looked at millions of tweets and showed their results in a webinar entitled "The Science of Timing," the later you tweet in the day, the better. The reason is that from 2PM to 5PM ET your followers are more likely to see your tweet because there are fewer things demanding their attention. In fact, 4PM was deemed to be the best time of the day. Zarrella also found that weekends are great for tweet attention as people are more relaxed and aren't conflicted by work.

Finally, Zarrella has also put together a nice page called TweetWhen that will analyze your last 100 tweets and tell you when the best times for you to tweet are. Here are some other stats about tweet timing:

- The most click-throughs come between 1 to 3PM EST Monday through Thursday.

- Not much happens after 8PM weeknights.

- Peak traffic time is from 9AM to 3PM EST Monday through Thursday. That doesn't necessarily mean that you'll get more responses though, since there's already a lot more competition for attention.

I have personally found that the best times for me to tweet are 9AM, 11AM, 2PM, and 5PM ET on weekdays. I've also found that 9AM, 11AM, 1PM and 4PM can be effective on the weekends, although Sunday is better for engagement than Saturday.

That said, Twitter is a dynamic medium that should be used that way. If there's something exciting happening, it might not always be possible or wise to wait for the so-called best times to tweet. There are certain announcements, like for a gig or a song release, that work best if they're scheduled for the best time of the day, and these are the ones that you time to make sure you get the most people viewing.

Scheduling Tweets

Since there are posts that work best if they're scheduled for the best times of the day, it's important to find a way to do that without disrupting your life. That's where a scheduler comes in. As with Facebook, posting your tweets at the right time is an crucial component in how many people you reach. And like Facebook, it's probably not feasible that you'll be available at exactly 4PM to send that tweet out. That's why it's vital that you schedule your promotional tweets, and once again there are many ways to do that.

All of the social media schedulers mentioned in the previous chapter work just as well for Twitter as they do for Facebook. In fact, it's very efficient to be able to schedule everything in one app, and that's exactly what we're trying to do - keep the time spent on mundane social tasks down to a minimum.

While a scheduler makes it possible to send the exact same message to Twitter and Facebook, that can cost you followers either on Twitter or Facebook as no one wants to see the same post repeated on different social networks. It is okay if you slightly change the post though, as that will get you double exposure without it feeling too overbearing.

TIP: If you post a tweet on Facebook, make sure that you don't use a shortened URL or include the hashtags.

Twitter Measurement

As with everything online, it's possible to measure how well you're doing on Twitter, although the measurement details can sometimes raise some eyebrows because of the differences in results between measurement tools. That's why it's best to look at the trends more than any actual scores that the following services provide. If you see a metric suddenly jump up or down, you want to know why. Likewise, if you see something trending up or down month over month, then it's time for some real analysis. Here are a few measurement services to check out.

- **Twitter Analytics:** Within Twitter you'll find some basic analytics that aren't very deep, but are useful in a broad sense. It lets you see the trends in number of tweets, followers, impressions, mentions and profile visits on monthly summary (see Figure 7.2).

Figure 7.2: Twitter analytics.

- **Klout**: Klout gives you a score based upon the total action from your Twitter, Facebook, Google+, Foursquare, Instagram and Linkedin accounts. You're able to see the approximate number of mentions, retweets, followers and lists you receive, as well as a 90 day history.

- **Trackur**: Trackur is another tool that provides social influence and sentiment analysis for a price. It looks at all social platforms, not just Twitter.

- **Kred**: Kred is pretty cool in that it looks at your entire social community and scores you on your influence. It gives you a 30 day follower count, shows influence and outreach, and shows your top locations and communities, among other things. You can also look at the Kred scores of others globally, check out the scores for books, movies and TV shows, and see what your friends are scoring. It's free for now.

Useful Twitter Tools

Here are a couple of helpful Twitter tools that can help you get a handle on social media management. These tools are free and easy to use.

- With **Tweriod**, timing Is everything. Just like with all your other social tools, when used for promotion, you want to send tweets at a time when they'll reach the most people. Tweriod analyses the tweeting habits of your followers, then suggests the best time for you to tweet.

- **Tweetstats** analyzes your tweets over time and is a good way to look at your personal stats in a nice graph.

Social media can be time consuming so anything that helps relieve that burden a bit is welcome to most of us. Try these tools out to make your Twitter promotional experience a little more efficient and easier.

Using Contests To Increase Your Followers

Photographer Scott Bourne uses an old idea to increase his Twitter followers by frequently holding a contest to win a high-end Canon camera. All you have to do is follow him on Twitter, and send out only a single tweet regarding the contest.

Scott asks his contest entrants to tweet only once in order to observe Twitter etiquette and avoid spam, and is very careful to spell that out on his entry page. He's also careful to spell out any possible problems that might occur either because of the entrants location or ethics.

The contest is a very clever use of social media, but it's clearly only part of Scott's strategy. He wants to raise his follower numbers, then be able to market to those followers later. He might not even want to directly market to them, instead just informing them and keeping them close as fans and market to them through his web site or blog. Either way, the contest is a winner.

Twitter Rules For Contests

As you can see, Twitter contests don't have to be elaborate to work. Contests and sweepstakes on Twitter can offer prizes for tweeting a particular update, for following a particular account, or for posting updates with a specific hashtag with no problems. Twitter does have some simple guidelines to follow though. Here are some things to include when setting the rules for your contest.

- **Discourage the creation of multiple accounts.** Some people want to win a contest so badly that they'll create dozens of accounts in order to enter. If found out, this can get them suspended, so it's best to include a rule in your contest stating that anyone found to use multiple accounts to enter will be ineligible.

- **Discourage posting the same Tweet repeatedly.** Posting duplicate, or near duplicate, updates or links is a violation of the Twitter Rules because it jeopardizes search quality. Don't set rules to encourage lots of duplicate updates (like saying, "whoever Retweets this the most wins"). You might want to set a clear contest rule stating that multiple entries in a single day will not be accepted.

- **Ask people to mention you in their update so you can see all the entries.** When it comes to picking a winner, you'll want to see all the contestants. If the updates mention you, you'll be able to see all the updates in your Notifications timeline. Simply running a public search may not show every single update, and some contestants may be filtered from search for quality.

- **Encourage the use of topics relevant to the contest.** You might decide to have people include relevant hashtag topics along with the updates (like #contest or #yourbandname). Keep in mind that hashtag topics need to be relevant to the update, and encouraging users to add your hashtag to totally unrelated updates might cause them to violate the Twitter Rules.

- **Follow The Twitter Rules.** While these guidelines should help keep your contest entrants in good standing, please make sure you also review both the Twitter Rules and our search best practices before starting your contest. Since you're really considered a business on Twitter, you might also want to check out business.twitter.com for more information and tips.

- **Applicable Laws and Regulations.** Before starting any contests or sweepstake, make sure it complies with all applicable laws and regulations. Compliance with these laws and regulations is your responsibility, and it's best to consult with an attorney if you have any legal questions.

20 Twitter Tips And Tricks

Now that you've read about all the ins and outs of Twitter, let's summarize with 20 tips and tricks:

1. Set up your profile. Your bio should include who you are and what you tweet about.

2. Be sure to use a photo of you, not a baby picture, celebrity or avatar.

3. Include your website or blog link in your profile.

4. Use fewer than 120 characters in any tweet for greater response.

5. Place a link in every tweet.

6. Don't use more than two hashtags per tweet.

7. Stay away from bashtags or anything negative.

8. Use link shorteners like Bit.ly, Tinyurl, or Ow.ly to make more room for text and links.

9. Use a Twitter client like Hootsuite or Tweetdeck to see all your Twitter feeds in one place and obtain Twitter analytics.

10. Don't worry about your number of followers. If your content is good, they will come.

11. Find your favorite brands/bands/artists/companies on Twitter and follow them. Tweet them your feedback.

12. Find people talking about your band, music or brand and follow them.

13. If someone mentions your brand/company/you, be sure to respond.

14. Set up Google Alerts for topics of interest to tweet.

15. Tweet live from gigs and events. Tweeting from events keeps your followers and positions you as an expert.

16. Balance tweets, replies and retweets. Too much of a good thing is too much.

17. Tweet photos. A picture is worth a thousand words.

18. Don't feed the trolls. You'll always find a person who wants to pick a fight. Don't get in the ring.

19. Whenever someone mentions you, add them to a "Fans" list. Follow them closely and tweet them separately about gigs, videos and song releases.

20. If you use Hootsuite, create a search stream for any mentions of your band, song or video, including any misspellings.

TIP: Make sure that you add a "Follow Me" Icon to all your online pages to give people outside of Twitter a chance to follow you.

8

Marketing With Instagram

According to Nielsen Research, if you want want to reach music lovers, Instagram is one of the best platforms to use for promotion.

Why? First of all, Instagram users are huge music fans, and spend 42% more money on music and listen 30% more than the general population. In fact, the typical Instagram user spends a surprising $269 per year on music, which is more than twice as much as the average music fan that subscribes to a streaming service.

This is all well and good, but if you don't know for sure if a large number of your fans are already on Instagram, then don't commit to it if you don't have time. Like on all other platforms, consistency is king so you have to be able to spend time on Instagram every single day for it to be promotionally successful. This might not be so easy, especially when you're already spending time on other social media platforms.

If you do decide to go ahead and market on Instagram, be aware of your brand before you begin to post. You want it to be consistent with your other online properties in terms of look, feel and attitude. This is one case where copying another artist who's successful might not be a good idea.

- **Don't just post a picture, try to tell a story with your caption.** Like with YouTube, you can't ignore the captions of your images, because the copy gives context to them. They also give you a way to tie an image back to your music.

- **Don't forget that Instagram is a great platform for contests.** A contest might ask users to comment on your photo, share it, mention a certain number of friends, or even share their own photo with a specific hashtag. Many users see these contests as one of the benefits of following an artist or band on Instagram, so don't worry about bothering people. Try one out, track the analytics, and see how it benefits your brand.

- **Consider collaborating with a popular Instagrammer or influencer in your genre of music or part of the music business.** Let them control your account for a day, or ask them to share their thoughts on your music. This could result in exposing your brand to their following and getting more followers as a result. Be aware that some people, artists or brands with big followings actually charge for this, but many want the same exposure as you to to increase their audience too.

Instagram Best Practices

There are a number of best practices to follow in order to build an Instagram community.

- **Your profile picture and description are important.** Make sure to include a profile picture that reflects your band or brand (a logo would be nice), and include a link to your website.

- **Shorten the Links With A URL Shortener.** Instagram's bio description has a limit of 150 characters, so it's important to save as many characters as you can. URL shorteners do what their name suggests: shorten links.

- **Leave Relevant Comments.** Comments are much appreciated by the poster because they're few and far between. For instance, every second on Instagram produces 575 "Likes" but only 81 comments. It's a lot easier to just click the like button, but comments get you followed back.

- **Use the filters.** Believe it or not, filters actually make a difference in engagement. For instance, a study of 6 million posts across 10,000 brands found that posts using Hefe, Lo-Fi, Nashville, Brannan, and Kelvin filters generated 4.5% to 5.6% more engagement than the average Instagram post!

- **Post at the correct times.** Mondays and Thursdays tend to drive the most engagement, while between 3 and 4PM typically drives lower engagement during a workday.

- **Also, like with other social networks, the number of times you post per day on Instagram is important.** It's been found that the ideal number is only one to two times per day. You can get away with more on special occasions like an event, but be sure to space out the posts so you don't overflow your followers feeds.

What Not To Do On Instagram

Like all other platform, Instagram has both a common etiquette and some things that violate the terms of service. Following these hints will attract the right followers and share the right content. Here are some things to consider:

- **Don't flood your follower's feeds with too much of the same thing**. You want your followers to anxiously await your posts, but that's not going to happen if they're bored or annoyed by too many photos that are not relevant. Pace your posts to keep your followers happy, but if you are going to post a flurry of photos, make sure you notify them in advance that it's going to happen.

- **Don't take credit for an image that isn't yours.** Don't steal images and pass them off as your own. If you share an image, be sure to give the creator credit by @mentioning them in the description of the post. Using others images is a great way to meet other users on Instagram, but you have to do it the right way.

- **Don't make irrelevant comments on other's images.** Remember that all comments are public and are shown on other people's feeds as well.

- **Don't ramble or get off-topic with your descriptions.** Be respectful of your followers. Keep the descriptions to the point.

Also, **your account can get shut down** if you do any of the following:

1. You share photos that show nudity.
2. You share photos of illegal content.
3. You spam others.
4. You're rude.
5. You abuse, attack or harass others
6. You promote or glorify self-harm.

Sometimes we can get into trouble by doing something without knowing what people consider accepted behavior, but if you follow the guidelines above, you should never have that problem.

How To Build Your Instagram Audience

You're on Instagram both to build your audience and inform them about what you're doing. Since you can't inform them until they follow you, here are a number of things that you can try to build your audience on the platform.

#1: Include A Call To Action

A call to action is asking your viewer to do something. That's called engagement and it's the key to building your audience. The best way to do this is just by asking them. A simple way to get more engagement is to ask followers to "tag the person you love most" in the caption, and they will likely tag others in the comments.

#2: Leverage Relevant Hashtags

Hashtags are a great way for artists to stand out on Instagram and find people who are not yet following their account. They help organize and categorize images, which aids in the process of content discovery. Just make sure to use Instagram hashtags that are relevant to the audience you're attempting to reach. We'll look at hashtags in depth in an shortly.

#3: Do Shout-outs for Shout-outs

On Instagram, you might notice people commenting on your photos with the acronym S4S (see Figure 8.1), which stands for shout-out for shout-out. A shout-out is when you promote someone else's account to your own followers.

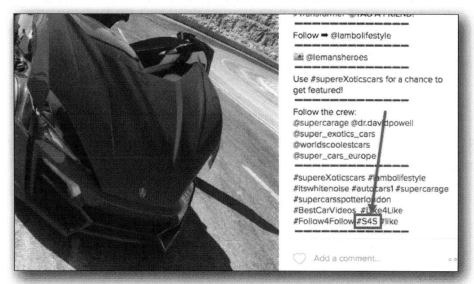

Start by looking for pages with a similar target audience so it's a mutually beneficial situation. To find these accounts, type keywords in the Instagram user search or do a web search for your specialty or musical genre plus "Instagram accounts." Add a caption asking if the user is interested in doing a shout-out for shout-out. When this user writes back, Instagram will let you know through a home screen notification.

Another version of that is #L4L or "Like for Like" meaning you say you'll like the posts of those like yours. #follow and #followme are other top picks, as is #photooftheday.

#4: Vary Caption Length

Each Instagram post allows 2,000 characters for captions, and the more of them you use, the more likely your post will be engaged. This is very similar to YouTube, where the description is critical to the video being found in a search.

#5: Interact With Other Users' Content

Interaction with other users posts gets you followers. A good way to find users with similar tastes to you is to do a search for some of the hashtags that you use. Engage with the users who are sharing content with this tag.

#6: Promote Your Account on Other Networks

As with other social networks, promoting your account on the other platforms that you use can be a big boost for your following. It's a quick and easy, and passive way to do this, and all it takes is setting it up one time and you're done.

Hashtags: The Key To Instagram Promotion

Hashtags are an essential part of Instagram marketing and promotion, so it's important that you're familiar about how they work on the platform.

Contrary to all other networks, on Instagram, the more hashtags you use, the better. That's because hashtags are the primary way you build a community on the platform. Believe it or not, between 7 and 11 hashtags get the most engagement, according to most studies.

That said, make sure you do some research as to which hashtags you'll use. Hyper-focused hashtags will put your images in front of a more interested audience. That means that you should use hashtags relevant to music, and to your music and brand in particular.

Three ways to search for new hashtags include hashtagify.me, websta.me/search, or picodash.com. Some of the most popular music related hashtags include:

#music	#musicman
#musician	#musicismylife
#musicians	#musicianlife
#musicproducer	#musicmonday
#musicvideo	#musicstudio

The best hashtags for getting new followers are:

#love	#follow
#instagood	#followme
#me	#photooftheday
#tbt (Throwback Thursday)	#happy
	#tagforlikes
#cute	

TIP: *Don't forget to include a custom hashtag of you or your band, if your following is large enough, and consistently use it on all your posts.*

Hashtags constantly change in popularity depending upon the current trends, so make sure you do regular searches just to be sure that you're using the best ones for your posts.

Marketing With YouTube

9

If a picture is worth a thousand words, then a video is definitely worth a heck of a lot more. That's why YouTube is one of the most powerful networks available for marketing an artist, band, or brand.

YouTube has the ability to visually reach so many people in such a short amount of time that you can almost consider it as a social "force multiplier" (to use a military term) that grows in power every day. As an example, it wasn't that long ago (2009) that singer Susan Boyle had a huge viral hit with what we thought at the time was enormous number of views at 100 million. Fast forward to 2012 and K-Pop singer Psy had the most widely viewed YouTube hit ever with more than 1.4 billion (yes with a B) in less than six months! While that song is now headed towards an incredible 3 billion views, even it has now been overtaken by Whiz Khalifa and Charlie Puth's "See You Again." In fact, over 10,000 videos have already accumulated over 1 billion views each!

Chances are good that you'll never hit that number of views, but there's also a very good chance that someone might discover your music on YouTube. After all, it's the #1 place after radio where people discover new music.

That's why YouTube is essential to an artist's social strategy, but there's a lot more to it than posting a video and hoping that it will go viral. Indeed, having that happen is like winning the lottery, but in reality, a video doesn't have to have a million views to be effective. Let's look at the various tips and tricks used to make YouTube an outstanding promotional tool.

YouTube By The Numbers

YouTube is a huge behemoth of a network that's grown far beyond anyone's expectations. The following numbers come from YouTube itself and are quite staggering:

- The total number of people that use YouTube is over 1.3 billion.

- 80% of YouTube traffic comes from outside the US.

- Over 5 billion videos are viewed a day.

- 300 hours of video are uploaded to the service every minute.

- Over 3 billion hours of video are watched each month on YouTube.

- More video is uploaded to YouTube in one month than the three major US networks created in 60 years.

- YouTube mobile gets over 1 billion views a day.

- 100 million people take a social action on YouTube (*likes, shares, comments, etc*) every week.

Music Discovery On YouTube

According to Accustream iMedia Research, 38.4 percent of YouTube's 1 trillion views were music videos, while streaming services like Pandora reported 8.2 billion hours of radio, Spotify 37 billion, and Rhapsody at around 7 billion.

That means the number of YouTube music views are larger than all other services combined. That's the best reason to place your songs on YouTube, because that's where people look first to find new music, at least currently. What's more, it doesn't have to be an expensive music video and it doesn't have to even be professionally made (although that helps a lot) to be effective.

TIP: A video with just the lyrics and the name of the artist as the song plays sometimes works just as well as a full-blown production. When it comes to music videos, the music still comes first.

Creating A YouTube Channel

Your YouTube presence is composed of both your YouTube channel and your individual videos. Having one without the other is an incomplete strategy that will cost you both brand identification and views. Therefore, if you haven't yet created a YouTube channel, or want to create a different one for your band, now is the time to create it.

YouTube now allows you to have two different kinds of channels, one for personal use and a "brand" channel. A brand channel is still accessed with a regular YouTube account but can use your band or artist name and can be managed by multiple people, meaning whoever you assign as channel owners and managers.

To create a channel, you have the option of doing so using a Google identity or creating a new account with a different username. If you have any kind of Google account, whether it be for Maps, Gmail or Google+, that's your Google identity. You'll use the same password that you normally use when signing into one of those products.

Let's say you want to create a brand channel for your band that's different from your personal channel. Here's what to do:

1. Sign in to YouTube on a computer or using the mobile site.

2. Go to your channel list by clicking on your channel icon in the top right corner of YouTube. Click the Settings wheel icon. Under "Account settings," click Overview.

3. Choose to create a new channel or use an existing Brand Account:

4. Create a new channel by clicking Create a new channel.

5. Create a YouTube channel for a Brand Account that you already manage by choosing the Brand Account from the list. If this Brand Account already has a channel, you can't create a new one—you'll just be switched over to that channel if you select the Brand Account from the list.

6. Fill out the details to name your new channel and verify your account. Then, click Done. This creates a new Brand Account.

Brand Accounts let you add owners and managers. Owners can add and remove other managers, remove listings, edit the business information, manage all the videos, respond to reviews, and more.

Managers can do all of those things except add/remove managers and remove listings, and communication managers can only respond to reviews and do a few other lesser managerial duties.

Here's how to add managers and owners:
1. Sign in to YouTube with the account that created the Brand Account (the one you created or logged in with above).

2. Click the account at the top right on YouTube and then choose the right channel from that list.

3. Click that area of YouTube again and then click the settings/gears icon to open the channel's account settings.

4. Click Add or remove managers from the "Managers" area.

5. Click the MANAGE PERMISSIONS button.

6. Choose the Invite new users icon at the top right of the Manage permission page.

7. Enter an email address that belongs to the user you want to add.

8. Choose a role for that user from the drop-down below the email address. Your options are Owner, Manager, and Communications manager.

9. Click INVITE.

TIP: Be sure to make a note of the URL so that you can send people to the channel later.

Optimizing Your YouTube Channel

Just like your Facebook and Twitter profile pages, a YouTube channel page is another opportunity to reinforce your musical branding. There's less flexibility in how you can brand that channel than there used to be, but there are still places where you can get creative.

Branding And Design

There are a number of areas that are available on your channel that enables you to emphasize your own design or brand. Let's look at them:

- **The Channel Art**: The channel art is the banner at the top of the page where you can display a customized graphic. YouTube suggests this graphic be 2560 x1440 pixels so that it works on all types of televisions, tablets, smartphones and computers, but what YouTube will show on most computer browsers is 1546 x 423. This is known as the "safe area" and is where you should place any critical graphics information since anything outside that area might not show up on a device with a smaller screen. The graphic can be up to 2MB and in either a JPG or PNG format. The Channel Art upload section is accessed by clicking on the pen icon on the top right of graphics box, as shown in Figure 9.1. You can access a template for the channel art, as well as a design tutorial, by clicking on "How to create channel art" at the bottom of the upload pop up box.

Figure 9.1: Accessing the Channel Art

- **The Channel Description:** You access your channel description from the *About* tab underneath your channel name. After the *About* box pops up, select the pen icon on the upper right to edit. From here you can enter or edit the description. Be sure to include all the information about your channel in the description, such as what to expect from the video content as well as who's involved (like the members of a band).

- **Website and Social Media Links**: The website and social medial links are accessed in the same manner as above; through the pen icon on the top right of the box. Here you can add links to websites, blogs and social networks (see Figure 9.2). The first weblink you entered will appear on the lower right side above your channel art, as will the social network icons. The others will appear in the *About* box.

Figure 9.2: The website and social media links editor

- **Channel Icon or Avatar:** The avatar is either a picture of you, your band, or product that appears on the upper left of your channel page. The avatar can be up to 800 x 800 (you're able to crop it) and 1MB in size, although the smaller the file size the better, since it will load faster. The picture is stored with your Google+ account, and you can also access any pictures stored there to use as your avatar.

- **Featured Video/Trailer:** Another thing that you can do is feature a particular video or trailer at the top of the page when someone who is unsubscribed visits your channel. Simply select the pen icon on the top right of the box, select a video, then hit save. You can see what both subscribers and non-subscribers see by toggling *Unsubscribed trailer* and *Subscriber view* next to the edit icon.

- **Playlists**: YouTube allows you to create multiple playlists, which can have a great influence in how your fans consume your content. If you have a fair number of videos, you might want to create different playlists for different parts of your fan base, since each may have a different desire of what to watch. While your superfans will want to see everything you upload, your casual fans may be more selective. You can select the order and layout of these playlists, or create a new one, by selecting the edit icon on the top right of the playlist box.

Channel SEO

There are a number of ways that you can optimize your channel so it's more friendly to search engines, which in turn will make it easier for people to find. Some of these are obvious, but others are not.

Your Channel Name

The way that most people, artists, bands and brands point viewers to their YouTube channels is by providing a simple URL that looks like this:

http://youtube.com/yournamehere

In my case, my YouTube channel is called polymedia (it's a long story why I don't use bobbyowsinski) so my URL looks like this:

http://youtube.com/polymedia

The problem with this is that both YouTube and Google searches actually look at it like this:

"http://youtube.com/user/yournamehere",
or my my case, "http://youtube.com/user/polymedia"

It seems like such a small thing, but if you add the "user" into the URL yourself, Google ranks your channel higher than if you don't use it. Thus for me:

"http://youtube.com/user/polymedia"
will rank higher than
"http://youtube.com/polymedia"

Reports are that people who have added the "user" to their URL's have jumped in rankings from in the 20's to the top 3. It doesn't look as nice, but if Google likes it better and will rank you higher, that's the way to go.

Custom URL

YouTube now allows you to add a custom URL to your channel, but there are some eligibility requirements. Your account needs to:

- Have 100 or more subscribers

- Be at least 30 days old

- Have an uploaded photo as channel icon

- Have uploaded channel art

In general, a YouTube channel may only have one custom URL and custom URLs cannot be transferred or assigned to anyone.

Once the eligibility requirements are met, set a custom URL by doing the following:

1. Go to your advanced account settings by clicking your icon in the top right > Settings or the wheel icon. Then click Advanced under your account name.

2. Under "Channel settings," select the link next to You're eligible for a custom URL. You'll only see this link if your channel is eligible.

3. In the "Get a custom URL" box, you'll see the custom URL(s) you've been approved for. You can't change the part in the gray box, but you may need to add a few letters or numbers to make the URL unique to you.

4. Carefully read and understand the "Custom URL Terms of Use" and select the box to agree to them, then click Change URL.

Once a custom URL has been approved, you can't request to change it, so make sure this is the custom URL you want before clicking Confirm choice.

TIP: Keep in mind that you can't change a custom URL after creation, including adjustments to the capitalization, accents, or diacritics. You can remove a custom URL from your channel up to 3 times per year. This deactivates the URL so that it no longer directs viewers to your channel.

Keywords

Your channel's keywords can be found in the *Advanced* tab under *Channel Settings* in the Video Manager (see Figure 9.3). Enter 5 or so keywords or keyword phrases that describe your channel, and separate them with quotes. While you're there, select "Allow my channel to appear in other channel's recommendations" so other channels can recommend you as well.

Figure 9.3: Channel keywords found in the Advanced section.

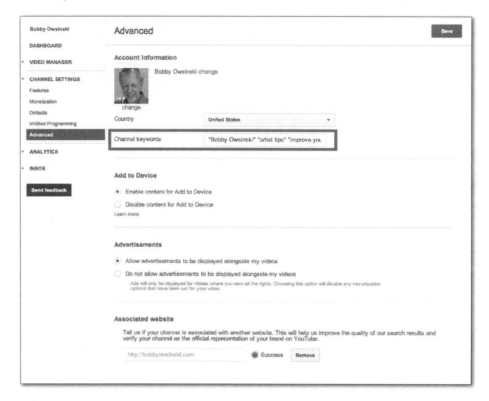

TIP: *Don't forget to include your artist or band name in the keywords.*

Feature Other Channels

Select "Feature Other Channels" in the *About* box in order to feature related channels on your channel. This is a great way to cross-promote with other similar artists to extend your reach and give your content some fresh ideas. Remember that the channels listed there are also listed as suggested channels when a user subscribes to your channel.

Optimizing Your Videos

There are a variety of ways to optimize your videos so they're easily found either by a Google search or YouTube search (which are basically the same thing since YouTube is owned by Google). While there's an entire science built around this, here are some easy basics that will get you most of the way there.

Video SEO Basics

Videos on any platform can be used as an effective marketing tool, but you must observe some essential SEO, or Search Engine Optimization, techniques for that to happen. Before you go live on a video, make sure that you do the following:

1. Name Your Video Something Descriptive. The title is the most important part of your video SEO. It has to be something that's short, easy to remember, and descriptive all at the same time, which isn't always easy to do. Let's look at a couple of *bad* examples first:

Bad Example: RrkSvle334.mov

Many video editing apps provide default names to movies that might make sense to a machine, but won't help anyone to find the video or know anything about it. The example above is one of those incomprehensible titles that violates the easy to remember and descriptive traits that we're looking for. Here's another bad example:

Bad Example: "The Unsigned Music Video"

Staying with our fake band The Unsigned, we can see that at least we know this video has something to do with the band, but we really don't have any idea about anything else. Here's a better title:

Better Example: "Tomorrow Today - The Unsigned"

This is much better because we now have the title of the song and the artist all in the movie title. This works pretty well for a music video, but what if the band was in the studio and shot a behind-the-scenes video? A mediocre title would be:

Bad Example: "The Unsigned In The Studio"

This is mediocre because it doesn't give us enough information. What was the band doing in the studio? What's the name of the studio? Here's a better way to title it:

Better Example : "The Unsigned Recording At La Grange Studios"

That gives the potential viewer a lot better idea of what the video is about. Sometimes even adding a date to the end can be helpful, although that also places an age on the video, which can be undesirable. That's not all we can do with the title though.

TIP: Don't make the title too generic (like "Music Video"), since it won't rank highly as a result. Do make it easy to spell, since it takes Google longer to learn it if it gets typed incorrectly during a search.

---

2. Choose Your Keywords Based On Your Title. One of the best things about the last title is that there are a lot of keywords in it that we can use as meta tags to make it easier to find. "The Unsigned," "Recording," and "La Grange Studios" are all keywords that we can use as tags, but we can improve the title a bit more with a few more descriptive keywords like:

"The Unsigned Recording Basic Tracks At La Grange Studios"
or
"Recording Basic Tracks At La Grange Studios - The Unsigned"

This is gives us a few more keywords that can be used as meta tags for SEO. Now every word except "At" is a keyword, which makes the title strong not only for the search engines, but for your fans to determine if this is something that they want to watch or not.

TIP: Put your most important keyword first in the title if possible.

---

3. The longer the description the better. One of the most overlooked portions of a video is the description (see Figure 9.4). Not only can this be loaded with pertinent information for the viewer to read, but search engines love it. Each description should contain a full "who, what, when, where and how" that completely explains the video and includes links to the website and social media. Anything from about 75 to 200 words works, although more is better, so don't be afraid to expand on the explanation and include the artist or band member's names, song title, album title, date recorded, date released, record label, and what happens during the video. Also don't be afraid to sprinkle in keywords where appropriate.

TIP: The correct ratio of keywords in your copy is around two to three percent, or two or three times every hundred words. A higher ratio may be considered "keyword stuffing" by the search engine and get you penalized with a lessor search ranking.

4. Make sure to include links in the video description. A video without links to your site is an opportunity wasted. You want the viewer to become a fan, so be sure it's easy for him to find more information by including a link to your website and/or social media.

TIP: Make sure that your description contains the same phrase as your title. Using our example above, that would mean "Recording basic tracks at La Grange Studios."

Figure 9.4: The video description

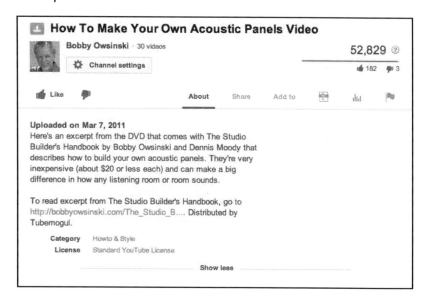

5. Add the proper tags. All of the keywords that you used in the title and description can be used as meta tags, although it's best to try to limit these to between five and seven. More tags aren't necessarily better, as these tags generally don't have that much effect on search ranking anymore anyway. One thing to remember is to make sure that all the major characters in the video are properly identified with tags. That said, misleading tags can cause YouTube to consider the video SPAM, which is something you don't want. You can add or edit tags by clicking on the *Info and Settings* icon (the first one) on the video viewer.

TIP: *YouTube now also makes tag suggestions, which you can select by just clicking.*

---

6. Create custom thumbnails for your videos. One of the easiest ways to get more views is by having an appealing thumbnail image. When you upload a video, YouTube usually selects three screen grabs from which you can select the thumbnail. The problem is that it's likely that none of these provide an image that instantly tells the potential viewer much about your video. A customized image can now be used as the thumbnail instead of the selections made by YouTube. Here's what to do:

- **Find the perfect still shot.** Search through your original video (the one you had before you uploaded it to YouTube) until you find that one shot that perfectly describes what the video is all about. This might be an action shot, or it could be a close-up of a face or product, or it could be anything that grabs the viewer's attention. Whatever it is, make sure that it's relevant to the video. When you've found it, export it as a jpeg or PNG image.

- **Add text.** Use an image editor like Photoshop, Pixelmator or GIMP to add text to identify the video. Make sure that the text is large enough to read easily on a small screen found on a smartphone. The file size should be less than 2MB.

- **Click on the *Custom Thumbnail* icon and upload.** This can be found on the *Info and Settings* page, which is accessible from the first icon (the first one) at the bottom of the video viewer. Viewers will now see your custom thumbnail.

7. Add a link. I'm sure you've seen videos that have embedded links to websites, social media and affiliate stores and wondered how that was achieved. Links can actually be added to a video in a number of ways. This involves the End Screen and Annotations feature, or the Card feature of your movie.

On the bottom left of the video viewer you'll see six edit icons. Go to the fourth one, which is *End Screen & Annotations*. Once you click on it, you'll see the End Screen editor, which will provide a timeline of your video, and on the right you'll see a blue bar that says *Add Element*. From there you can select a *Link* selection that will open up the Link window where you can program exactly when that link will appear and the duration it stays on the screen.

When adding a link this way you're limited to links that you designate within YouTube, such as a link to another video, a channel, playlist, subscribe, Google+ profile or fundraising project, or what's known as an "associated website." You can have multiple associated websites.

In order to designate an associated website:

1. Click on the *Channel Settings* icon below your channel name. It will take you to the *Advanced* settings tab.

2. Insert the URL of your associated site, then click verify.

3. After YouTube verifies that your site is real, the green "Success" button will light. You can now link to your associated website.

TIP: It's best if you use your website as the associated site, since that's usually where you want to send viewers.

---

8. Post socially. When you upload a video (or even after it's been uploaded), you can choose to share your video along with your comments to Google+, Facebook and Twitter directly from YouTube. That said, sometimes customized posts to your social networks have a much greater affect, so that's something that you might want to consider. Sharing is done on the lower right side of the video's *Info and Settings* page below *Post to your subscribers*.

9. Don't forget the contact info. Always be sure to add your contact info to the end of the video. Even if it's just a website URL, you can't always be sure where someone will view the video, so it's best to have that additional info at the end so that the viewer can get more info if he wants it.

10. Embed your videos. Why have a link that takes people away from your blog or site when you can easily keep them there in the first place? With YouTube, it's so simple to embed a video these days. Just click on the *Share* button beneath the video, then the *Embed* button, copy the code, then paste it into the HTML of your blog or website. It's easy and almost no hassle, since you don't have to worry about uploading a video or any bandwidth limitations that might be imposed by your ISP.

TIP: Make the video for yourself first. If you're not having fun and enjoying the process, it will come through the camera to your viewers.

Video Branding

YouTube now allows you reinforce your channel branding by placing a custom thumbnail watermark on every one of your videos. Go to the YouTube *Video Manger* link, then click on *Channel* and you'll find *Branding* as an option. If you want it to look like the logo bug that you see on television, the watermark should be transparent and 800 pixels by 800 pixels. The file format can be JPG (remember that JPG doesn't support transparency), GIF, BMP or PNG, but make sure that it doesn't exceed 1MB.

While this branding feature might work in some cases, other times your viewers might think it's excessive. It is convenient though, in that you're able a watermark to all your uploaded videos at once.

The Key To Viral Videos

Everyone would love for their video to be like Whiz Khalifa's "See You Again" and go viral with millions of views overnight, but that rarely happens. That said, there are a number of generally accepted principles for creating a video that has a chance to go viral:

- **Keep it short.** It seems pretty obvious, but videos have a much better chance of going viral if they're short, mostly because that's what our attention span demands these days.

- **Provoke a response**. You'll see that most viral videos cause you to laugh or gasp. Anything else and your viewers probably aren't going to want to share it with their friends.

- **Be timely.** You have a greater chance to go viral if your content is about something currently popular, although there are perennials like cats and babies that never seem to go out of style.

- **Try humor to keep your viewer's interest**. That said, don't force it since that can be most unfunny.

- **Avoid asking for comments.** One thing that turns people off is asking them to like, share or comment on the video. If they enjoy your video they'll do all of these things naturally and won't need to be cajoled.

- **Don't create a commercial.** Viral videos are hard enough to create, but they're even more difficult if they're constructed like ads. It's true that you're creating a video to promote either an album, a song or your band, but being subtle works best.

- **Avoid Copyrighted Material.** Copyrighted material can stop a video dead in its tracks due to a take-down notice from the content owner's attorney. You might get away with it; then again, you might not.

- **Seed your content.** Before your video can go viral, you've got to get it in front of influencers. Consider using a viral seeding company such as Sharethrough to do that for you. Be aware that these services usually charge a per view fee so the costs can rack up, but it's measurable and effective with the right video.

- **Don't create a video because you think it might get views.** Create content that you really care about.

- **Watch other videos for inspiration and tips.** You can learn a lot about what to do, and maybe more importantly, what not to do, from other artists, bands and brand's videos.

- **But be yourself.** You're better at being you than anyone else.

Don't Believe The Half-Life

Even though we'd all like the next huge viral hit, having a viral video isn't the key to promotion after all. Sometimes a clever promotional video that isn't viral in the slightest can be just as effective (or even more so) in getting the word out.

While a study by video distributor TubeMogul (now sadly out of business) found that a typical YouTube video gets 50% of it's total views within the first six days and 75% of the total views after 20 days, the study mostly applied to DIY "novelty" videos, and not to those that are meant to extend your brand. The fact is, many videos gradually gain an audience and continue to build over time, especially after a mention on a blog or social network. Many of the videos on my own YouTube (youtube.com/polymedia) channel are good examples. They'll have a slow first week or month or even a number of months, then they gradually pick up steam.

Optimizing Video For Mobile

Mobile viewers watch videos a lot longer than they do on their desktops. In order to maintain that attention, it's important to observe the following:

1. Avoid using tiny text. Make sure that any text you use is readable on any screen that the video might be viewed on, especially a smartphone.

2. Make sure the audio is clear. Great audio is always a plus, but even more so when viewing on a phone. Remember that the speakers are small, so you're not going to hear many of the low frequencies, but that's okay as long as everything is intelligible. Also remember that there's always a lot of ambient noise around a phone if the user isn't wearing earbuds, so make sure that the audio is able to cut through it.

3. Use lots of close-ups. Close-up shots work great on small screens - wide shots don't.

4. Test the video on your own phone before you upload it. What good is the video if it doesn't get the point across? The only way you'll know for sure is if you test it, and your personal phone is a great place to start.

These are all good tips to keep in mind the next time you create a video. Remember that it's more than likely that a great number of your viewers will now be watching on their phone, so compensate for the small screen right from the beginning.

People Watch Longer On Tablets

While most people watch at least a couple of YouTube videos on their laptop or desktop during the day, it turns out that tablet users actually have the longest video engagement. Video distributor Ooyala did a study that determined that tablet users watched 28 percent longer than the desktop average. They also found that tablet viewers are more than twice as likely to finish a video than on a desktop, which was about 30 percent higher than that of mobile devices.

The study also found that desktops and laptops are more likely to be used for short video clips, whereas videos that are 10 minutes or longer make up 30 percent of the hours watched on mobile devices, 42 percent on tablets, and nearly 75 percent on connected TV devices and game consoles.

The bottom line is, if you make a video, be sure that it plays well on a tablet.

Making Money From Your Videos

Many artists, bands, brands and videomakers are using YouTube to generate income. The majority of the time this is done through a version of Google's Adsense program, which allows publishers in the Google Network of content sites to serve automatic text, image, video, and rich media adverts that are targeted to that particular site's content and audience. YouTube's monetization features are very easy to apply, so let's take a look.

Enabling Your Account

The first thing to do is enable your account for monetization. This is done under the *Channel* link and then clicking *Monetization*, at which point you'll be lead through the registration process (see Figure 9.5).

You will not be able to monetize your channel and videos until your channel reaches a total of 10,000 views!

Figure 9.5: Monetizing your account

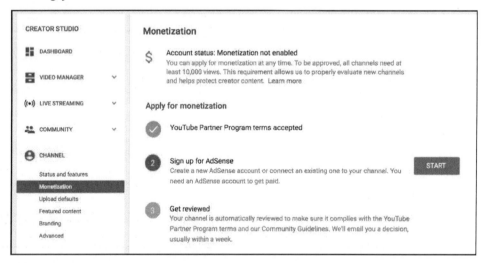

After your application for Adsense is confirmed, click on the *Start Monetizing Your Videos* link and you'll be taken to your video manager, where you'll be able to see a list of your uploaded videos.

To the right of each video in the Video Manager you'll see three small tabs; the first selects whether the video is available to the public or only private viewing, the second shows when the video was published, and the third (the one with the dollar sign) will allow you to monetize the video. When you click on the monetize tab a new window with your video will load with a selection box at the bottom that says *Monetize my video*. Once that's selected, a new set of selections appear.

TIP: *Be sure your video has at least a PG-13 rating if you want to appeal to advertisers to make monetization possible.*

Selecting The Ad Type

Now you're able to select the type of ads and the way they show up in your video (see Figure 9.6). The first is *Overlay Ads* which loads a transparent ad bar on the lower portion of the video. This is usually the most unobtrusive type of ad, since it allows the user to instantly play your video without having to wait for a commercial to start.

Figure 9.6: Ad type selections

The next choice is *Sponsored Cards*, where viewers will see a teaser for the sponsored card which lasts just a few seconds. They can then choose to click on the Card icon that appears in the top right-hand corner of the video they are watching to access further information about the sponsored content.

Last is *Skippable video ads.* This is the dreaded pre-roll commercial that occurs before your video begins. The viewer has the choice of skipping to your video after five seconds, but that also means that the advertiser doesn't have to pay much when that happens, which also means you don't get paid much either.

You can also choose where the ads appear using the Ad Breaks tool at the bottom of the page (see Figure 9.6). There you can select the ad to be inserted before the video begins, or anywhere in the video, or have YouTube suggest placement for you by select on the box on the bottom.

The ads in your video are chosen automatically based on the context of the video, which includes the demographic of the viewers, the title and metadata, and how you categorize your video. This means that if you have a music video, the ad is probably going to relate to the person who likes music. You're not able to manually select the type of ads that are inserted at this time.

What's more, once you've been selected to be an Adsense partner, banner ads sized at 300 pixels x 250 pixels will also appear on all pages but your channel homepage. This may or may not be related to the ad in the video. It's possible to filter or block Adsense banner ads that appear next to your video though, and you can block either by advertiser URL or by category. To do this you have to log in to your Adsense account and visit the *Allow and Block Ads* tab, which is beyond the scope of this book.

One of the things about ads is that they appear even if you or someone else embeds your video on another site, which allows you to still generate income even if the video isn't on a site that you control.

TIP: Don't expect to make a huge amount of money from ads in your video. The average ranges from between around $600 to $1,200 per million views (although it may be higher). On top of that, YouTube may ask you to prove that you own or control the copyright of the material on the video before monetization can begin.

How Video Views Are Counted

Video views are an important measurement for not only artists and bands, but record labels, advertisers and sponsors. A high number of views can lead to not only to label and sponsor interest, but also has a snowball effect of more viewers wanting to watch as well. When it comes to monetizing video views though, the problem is that most services like Facebook, YouTube, Instagram, Twitter and Snapchat all measure what they consider a "view" differently.

Here are 4 factors that determine a view:
1. Whether the video autoplays or was user initiated
2. The amount of time spent watching the video
3. The amount of video that's on the screen
4. Whether the video is played in the app or embedded in another site

Let's look at what the qualifications for a view are on some popular platforms:

- Facebook is the most liberal with what it considers a view. If a video is autoplayed for just 3 seconds, and it's 100% on the screen for desktop or 50% for mobile, it's considered a view.

- For Snapchat, as soon as a video is played, even with autoplay, it's considered a view if it's 100% in view and played in the app.

- With Instagram, if the video is played for 3 seconds either in the feed or upon opening a story, and it's 100% in view in the app only, it's considered a view.

- For Twitter, the video can be autoplayed, and as long as it's watched for 3 seconds and is 100% in view either on mobile or desktop, it's considered a view. This counts across all platforms and embedded posts as well.

- YouTube is much tougher than any of the above. The video has to be user initiated, and it has to be viewed an indeterminate % of the total video length. For advertisers, it has to be 50% in view, but that includes all devices, all platforms, and embedded posts.

As you can see, not all views are equal and some of the view numbers you see can be taken with a grain of salt as a result.

How Video Views Are Monetized

First of all understand that just because your video is being viewed doesn't mean that you're getting paid. Your channel must first be signed up with Google Adsense (who supplies the adverts), then set for monetization, then the monetize option for each video must be selected. It's only at that point that your videos can begin to be monetized.

View Variables

There's more to it than that though, as with everything involving digital music. The commercial on the pre-roll must be watched all the way through or else it doesn't count towards monetization. If there's a banner ad across the bottom of the video, it must be viewed for at least 31 seconds before it counts as a monetized view.

There's also the fact that YouTube doesn't sell ads on all of your views. Then some views on mobile devices just don't register unless the viewer uses an official YouTube app.

Another major factor is the advertiser and the type of ad that's placed on your video. If your audience happens to like expensive cars, jewelry or clothing, then an advertiser would probably be willing to pay a higher ad rate, which means that each video view would earn more money.

Yet another variable is the time of year the video is viewed, as many advertisers pay more for the holiday season than in January, for instance.

And then there's the type of ad that's used on the video or channel. This can vary from a skippable video ad that runs before your video begins (a "pre-roll"), to a transparent overlay add that takes up the bottom portion of your video, to a display ad featured to the right of your video and more. Each pays at a different rate.

That's why there's a wide range of payouts that can go anywhere from around $1.50 to $8.00 per thousand views. That means that a monetized video with 1 million views may generate anywhere from $1,500 to $8,000. YouTube takes a 45% cut however, which then puts the income to the copyright holder to between $825 and $4,440 (and sometimes even less).

A generally accepted average of what to expect from a million video views is around $1,750, or $0.00175 per view after the split with YouTube, although its also common to see payouts as low as $0.006, or $600 per million views.

Don't forget that if you're signed to a record label, that this is what the label takes in, and you're paid at your label royalty rate (15 to 25% of the net amount) minus any recoupable deductions. No wonder why you're not seeing any YouTube money."

How Content ID Can Earn You Money

In 2007 YouTube created the technology used to detect uploaded videos that infringe on copyright called Content ID. This creates an identification file for copyrighted audio and video material and stores it in a database. When a video is uploaded, it's checked against the database and flags the video as a copyright violation if a match is found.

When this occurs, the content owner is alerted, and then has the choice of blocking the video to make it unviewable, allowing the video to be viewed while tracking the viewing statistics of the video, or adding advertisements to the video and collecting the revenue.

To qualify for Content ID, you must own or control the exclusive online streaming rights for the content you upload. To sign up, go to youtube.com/content_id_signup.

Creating Online Video Contests

Artists, bands and musicians are always looking for ways to increase their fan engagement, and contests can be a good way to do that. A white paper from Launchpad6, a site that specializes in conducting all kinds of online contests, had a number of suggestions regarding conducting a successful one with video. The following three ideas from the paper are worth considering.

1. You need a premise. A premise is the basic idea of the contest itself. Here are some ideas to ask yourself first:

- Is content for the contest readily available or easily created?

- Is that content interesting?

- Is the content shareable?

- Is there enough passion for the idea?

- Is an element of voyeurism involved?

2. You need a prize. Cash is always king when it comes to attention, but sometimes smaller more niche prizes can be more alluring to your target audience. Ask yourself the following questions:

- Does the prize appeal to my target market?

- Will my market find the prize valuable?

- Are there any other smaller prizes that I can offer?

3. You need promotion. Your contest won't get any traction if it's not promoted and you get people to enter. Here are a few ideas to consider:

- Create a video for the contest and seed it around the web

- List your contest in directory sites

- Don't forget social media

- Try partnering with a blog or industry publication or anything that has more reach than you do.

Video Analytics

One of the best things about YouTube is that it has extensive analytics that allow you to measure the engagement of videos. These can be accessed either from the *Views* button located on the navigation bar at the top of your channel (see Figure 9.7) or through the Video Manager. Among the measurements that can be found are:

- The number of total channel views

- The estimated total number of minutes watched

- The total estimated earnings (provided that you've signed up for Adsense)

- The number of likes, dislikes, shares, shares, comments and favorites and subscribers added

- The location in the world where people are watching your videos

- The gender of your viewers

- Where people discover your videos

- The top traffic sources

Figure 9.7: Typical YouTube Analytics

Each one of the above is available in a separate report that allows you to look at a particular period in time, from a single day to the entire history of your channel. You can also look at these metrics for each single video as well.

Some of the most useful metrics are now available in the analytics on the left sidebar. You'll find some interesting metrics such as *Watch Time* and *Demographics* that can be very useful in determining just how effective each video is when it comes to engagement or making money.

TIP: *Use all the analytics and metrics available, not just views. Remember that it's the quality of views (meaning the length of time spent watching), not the quantity that's important.*

Tips For Increasing Your YouTube Engagement

Even though Facebook is catching up, YouTube engagement is still a primary concern for every artist. Information is power, and some brand new data about viewership on YouTube helps to maximize its usefulness as a promotional tool.

For instance, video length is one of the biggest deciding factors for engagement. Videos under one minute are watched to completion 80 percent of the time, while 2 to 3 minute clips have 60 percent retention rat and 5 to 10 minute videos are only completed 50 percent of the time.

Here are 5 tips for increasing YouTube engagement.

1. Focus promotion on mobile viewers. 98% of millennials watch video on their smartphones, and 92% of mobile viewers share videos.

2. Post and share at an appropriate time. The peak time for viewing on the smartphone, tablet or computer is between noon and 5PM.

3. Create videos that appeal to audience passions and align with your channel's brand. 67% of shoppers played a video with the idea of making a purchase and watched it at least 80% through. That means that a video introducing your latest merch or release can be very effective.

4. Increase shares and shelf life by embedding videos in emails. There's a 96% increase in click through rate, 26% fewer people unsubscribe, and 19% more people open when the title contains the word "video."

5. Collaborate with viewers and cultivate community. YouTube provides the option for crowdsources subtitles and closed captions in 60 different languages.

Remember that the average watch time for a video is 2.7 minutes. The longer a video drags on, the lower its retention, which is no surprise. The human attention span in 2015 was a mere 8.25 seconds (and 9 seconds for a goldfish).

YouTube is still the king of the mountain when it comes to video, so its best to pay attention to the latest statistics.

Using LinkedIn For Marketing

10

LinkedIn isn't usually one of the social networks that comes to mind when you're talking about audience building, promotion or marketing, but it can be a very powerful tool nonetheless. While all of those things can happen on LinkedIn, it's most useful to a musician, artist, band, engineer or producer by doing what it's good at, and that's connecting you with professionals that might be useful in running the business of your music.

For instance, maybe you're looking for a social media manager, or a video editor or a recording studio. LinkedIn's a great place to get access to a pro that might be invisible to you otherwise. Maybe you're looking for a manager, a music attorney or a promoter in Germany. There's no better way to contact the right person without having to wade through the different layers of people in your way if you cold called.

The best part is that the other person can check you out as well, If you present a professional image and have a complete description of your brand, you can get the seal of approval and provide the pro with some of your background before you even exchange a message.

There are actually a number of ways to connect people that you might want to do business with within LinkedIn, but the new ProFinder may be the easiest. It allows you to create a full proposal of what you're looking for, target the area of expertise that you need, and then have pros with that expertise bid on it. We'll take an in-depth look at ProFinder later in the chapter.

As for marketing your brand and music on the platform, it is possible to increase your fan base and mailing list, but don't expect numbers like on other social networks. We're talking more about business to business networking here, than business to consumer.

That said, it's a powerful platform that has over 460 million users, so don't underestimate it's reach.

Setting Up Your LinkedIn Profile

Probably the most crucial part of LinkedIn is your profile, since that will determine how how people will interact with you (see Figure 10.1). This is one time when looking cool might not be to your benefit, but looking more professional will. Let's look at some things to keep in mind.

Figure 10.1: A LinkedIn profile

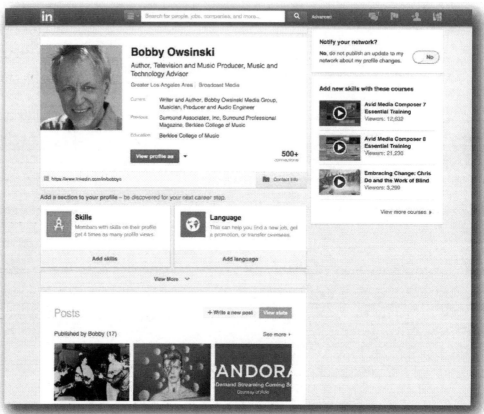

According to LinkedIn, adding a profile pic makes your profile 14 times more likely to be viewed by prospective clients, recruiters, and employers, but for our purposes that's actually beside the point. That said, the picture itself really makes a difference to anyone you're trying to connect with.

- **For one thing, use a recent photo.** That picture from 10 years ago just won't do, and neither will one that you use on a social network or a dating site. Make sure to use a professional photo. That's what everyone expects, and it sets up your brand.

- **The best pictures have solid color backgrounds with your face taking up as much of the frame as possible.** The image upload tool in LinkedIn includes a cropping feature to make this easier.

- **The Professional Headline that appears below your name is included on every reference about you on the site, so be sure it adequately describes you.** "Guitarist for the Unsigned band" or "Los Angeles mixing engineer" give the reader an instant idea of what you do with enough detail to not have to read the summary if they don't want to.

- **That summary section is sometimes the most overlooked section.** You have 2,000 characters to speak to your target audience and tell you story.

TIP: *It's been found that the summary connects with readers better if you write in complete sentences and in first person.*

- **Make sure that you add your contact info and a link to your website.** When filling in your URL you can select either *Blog* or *Website*, but if you want it to stand out, select the "*Other*" option. Now you can add your own website title and URL.

- **Key Words are incredibly important to your profile as this is a major way that people will find you when searching.** when search is a big part of the equation. Using the right keywords in your profile is the difference between being found and being invisible.

- **Identify the words you want to be found for** when people use LinkedIn search and use those keywords in your headline, summary, and profile.

- **Poor grammar, typos, and misspellings are a no-no on any platform, but especially on LinkedIn.** People expect a certain level of professionalism at all times so avoid them at all costs.

- **Don't forget to claim your custom URL.** Everyone should claim their custom URL to ensure it includes their name (e.g., http://linkedin.com/in/bobbyowsinski). Claiming your custom URL makes it more likely your LinkedIn profile will rank in the top of those search results.

- **Add more media.** LinkedIn now allows additional media to be added to your profile in the form of documents, photos and videos (see Figure 10.2). Consider adding a full artist bio as well as any photo or picture that you feel tells the story about what you do. Be careful not to add too much here since that will just cause the reader to move on without looking at anything.

Figure 10.2: Adding more media

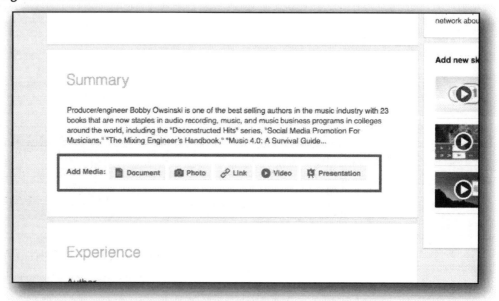

- **One final thing that you can do is to brand your profile page.** You can give it a bit more personality by adding a visually appealing background image (see Figure 10.3). LinkedIn advises users to use an image (PNG, JPG, or GIF) with a resolution of 1400x425.

Figure 10.3: Adding a background image

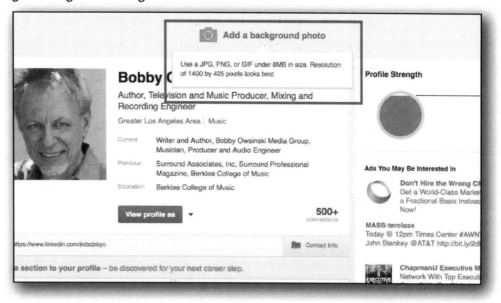

Follow these secrets and you'll find that LinkedIn will be well-worth being on.

LinkedIn Networking Tips

The key to being successful on LinkedIn is networking with people, and this platform may be the easiest way to connect with other people in your industry of anything available, and with high-level pros at that.

Who should you connect with? Basically anyone in the music industry. Let's start with industry leaders. Label execs, session musicians, musicians in other bands, studio owners, publishers, music attorneys, tech execs connected with the music industry - these are all valuable connections to have and a great place to start. Just do a search for any of those categories and see who pops up.

Journalists and bloggers are another group that you might want to reach out to. Normally they're difficult to connect with, since they're inundated with press releases and people asking for reviews. LinkedIn allows you to connect with them on more of an even basis than through a cold solicitation through an email or blog post.

People from industry conferences are another group that you can access via LinkedIn. If you've ever attended a conference like South by Southwest or an ASCAP Expo, you might have listened to some speakers that you found impressive and would like to connect with them. You can stand in line in an attempt to catch them after a panel, but even if you get that chance, you probably won't get much of their attention. Things are just too crazy at a conference. Finding them on LinkedIn later is much easier, and a better solution overall.

Ways To Find People

One of the great things about LinkedIn is that it really helps you connect with people. While you can do a search to find a specific person you're trying to reach, LinkedIn also offers other ways to make connections.

Upload Your Email List

You can upload your contact list to LinkedIn and it will make suggestions for new contacts based on your list (see Figure 10.4). LinkedIn calls this Contact Targeting, and it can be very effective if you already have some high quality contacts on your list.

Figure 10.4: Uploading your contact list

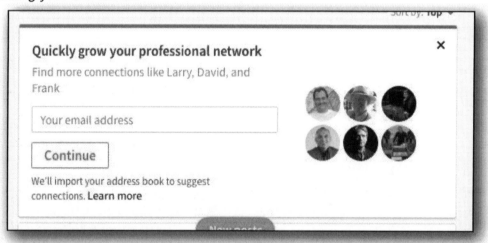

The People You May Know Tool

A great way to find people is to use the suggests from the People You May Know tool. This is a great way to find people that you already know and learn about people that you should know. The suggestions are based on your profile, so make sure that you've done a thorough job of adding your work and non-work experiences.

Join A Group

Another way to connect with people is to join an industry-oriented group. The key here is to contribute to the group by asking and answering questions. There are dozens of entertainment industry groups but a few to start with are:

- Music & Entertainment Professionals

- Music Industry Professionals

- Guitar Players, Bands, Musicians, Performers

- The Music Industry Forum

- The Audio Engineering Society

One way to find a group that's applicable is to look at the groups your connections are connected to. Here's how to do it.

1. Find influencers in your niche.

2. Scroll down in their profile until you find their LinkedIn groups. Join those that are relevant and sizable (you don't want a group that only has 10 people, for instance).

3. Add yourself to each group.

4. Join discussions or start the discussions.

Ask For Help

One of the best ways to connect with people on a more personal basis is to ask for advice. People rarely turn down a chance to help if they can. Just remember that most people (especially high-level pros) are really busy, so try not to waste their time by asking too many questions.

Remember, don't spam! That's the quickest way for you to get your account banned. Stay topical and humble and you'll find the help you need.

LinkedIn Posting Tips

One of the best LinkedIn marketing strategies is to write articles to post on the platform. Creating content allows you reach a new audience and make more connections, but it's very dependent upon your writing skills. People expect a lot on LinkedIn so don't attempt this if you not a good communicator.

Updates

Writing posts (or status updates) specifically for LinkedIn is the fastest way to grow your brand and connections on the platform. Just like a Facebook timeline, your post will appear in your connection's timelines and can be shared by your connections so that others outside of your direct network can read it. According to LinkedIn, posting 20 posts a month (or one every weekday) allows you to reach 60 percent of your audience, which is far more than Facebook, so you can see just how powerful this can be.

On your LinkedIn home page, just go to "Share an update" and you can select to share it with the public, with just your followers, or the public plus your Twitter feed (see Figure 10.5).

Figure 10.5: Adding a post

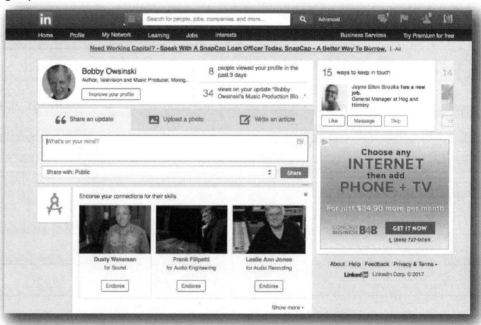

LinkedIn Pulse

Another thing that's very powerful is to publish articles on LinkedIn Pulse (see Figure 10.6). This is typically for a longer article the length of a blog post (300+ words) or more, so it's different from the shorter update. Use Pulse to generate leads by watching who likes and comments on your articles, then connect with them!

Figure 10.6: Posting on LinkedIn Pulse

One way to drive traffic from LinkedIn is to post partial articles and then link back to your site to read the rest. LinkedIn members may frown upon having to leave the platform, so do so with caution.

Post Updates With Images

This is typical for any social network and it also applies here (see Figure 10.7). Posts and articles with images get more views, likes and comments. Make sure you post an image that's relative to the article or post, and once again, the more dynamic the image, the better.

Figure 10.7: A Pulse article complete with graphic

Promote Your News

You can post your own news in groups and even link those news items back to any other websites you might have. Many members have weekly or even daily updates of group activity so your news will get delivered straight into their inboxes.

TIP: LinkedIn is not like Twitter. Posting several times a day might be too much for your connections. Also remember that LinkedIn is a business network, so it's best to use it during business hours.

Using ProFinder

While one way to find the connection to a professional service you need is through looking at your connections or doing a search, an easier way is to use LinkedIn's ProFinder marketplace. Here you can hire a freelancer for any number of services you might need, from graphic design to social media management services to video editing to accounting and taxes. You'll find ProFinder under the Work tab on your home page (see Figure 10.8).

Figure 10.8: Finding the ProFinder

There you can select from among 140 areas. Just fill in the details about your specific need and you'll receive up to five offers from freelancers with a message, price quote, and a link to their LinkedIn profile.

ProFinder doesn't cover as many things in the entertainment business as we'd like, but it does make it easy to find entertainment attorneys, photographers, social media managers, graphic designers, caterers and other services that musicians and artists often need. Best of all, there is no cost for this service either for you or for the freelancer.

The freelancers on ProFinder are vetted by a real person to weed the scammers out, so you can be pretty sure you'll get a real pro to take on your job.

The site will guide you through a proposal, but be sure to be as specific as possible in order to get the right person for the job.

11

Setting Up A Blog

A blog is one of the best ways to keep a consistent dialog with your existing fans while building a larger audience, and it's even possible to make some money at it as well. Blogging is an especially useful venture if you have strong opinions, are an expert at something, or have significant experience in an area. That said, building a successful blog does take time, and, like most other ventures online, depends upon how and when you do it.

Blogging Overview

A blog is an in-depth text broadcast. Think of it as talk radio, only with text. You broadcast your idea (a post on your blog), then if it catches the attention of enough readers, people respond and comment. Just like radio and television has Arbitron ratings to show how many people are tuning in, the number of page views each post gets is your ratings system.

Depending upon how serious you are about it, blogging can be a part of your online strategy in many ways. If you're a prolific writer who has a lot of expertise in a particular area (musicians have lots of expertise in music, travel and recording), you can share what you know. It can also be used as a way to keep fresh material on your website, or as a place for more extensive communication with your fans.

A blog is an excellent way to say a lot more than what's possible in any kind of social media. You have way more to say than the 140 characters Twitter makes available to you, and way more than what is appropriate for Facebook. Plus, a blog post is much more accessible than a YouTube video, since most people would rather graze through text then wait for a video to end.

Blogs also provide a greater ability than social networks to add graphics and photo galleries, the ability to have multiple pages of background material, and a way to easily access archives to your posts. Simply put, a blog doesn't replace another social media platform, but a social media platform can't replace a blog either.

Blogging Platforms

Right now there are five major blogging platforms; Wordpress, Blogger, Typepad, Medium, and Tumblr. While various website software packages have their own blogger tools that you can also use, the big 4 are specifically designed for blogging, and as a result they have more tools and provide far greater control than some blog add-ons that come with a website package. That's not to say that much of what we'll talk about won't apply if you're using a blog add-on to your website, since the essence of this chapter works on any platform, it's just that a dedicated blogging platform has a variety of advantages that are worth using when you're starting out.

Blogger

Blogger is owned by Google, is dead easy to set up and use, and is free. The service is hosted on Google's servers, has a number of attractive templates to choose from, and is easy to post and update. You can use the blogger URL (i.e. bobbyowsinski.blogspot.com) or have your own URL mapped over it (i.e. yoursite.com) for a $10 per year fee. There's also hundreds of widgets available that allow you to insert anything on your blog from the current local weather to eBay listings to the joke of the day in order to keep a steady stream of fresh content available.

Blogger was my personal blog of choice for the first five years of both my Big Picture production blog and Music 3.0 music industry blog, and I posted nearly 4,000 posts between the two (see Figure 11.1). The reason why I chose Blogger is that when I first started blogging, the platform felt the easiest of the the Big 3 blogging services (Tumblr wasn't available then). I'm not so sure that's the case today, but in the name of continuity and consistency (both of which are important blog qualities as you'll see), I stayed with it a little longer than I should have even though some of the others may offer more. A few years ago I moved to Wordpress because there was just more and newer design options available.

Figure 11.1: The Blogger post entry page

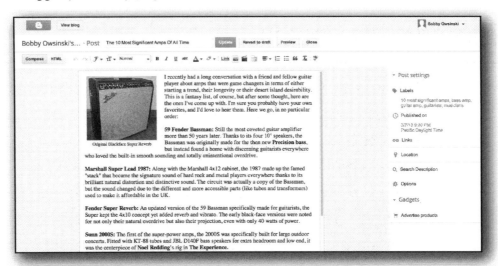

Wordpress

Wordpress is the most popular blogging platform in the world with over 75 million users, a number that continues to grow thanks to the constant improvement of its many features. In fact, the platform now powers 26% of all the sites on the web, including sites and blogs from TED, NBC, TechCrunch, CNN and the NFL, among others. It has a bigger set of features, templates and widgets than the other blog platforms, and it's also possible to host it directly on your server instead of using the Wordpress host service (see Figure 11.2).

The way this works is that anything that's "consumer" oriented is hosted at Wordpress.com and has a wordpress.com extension (i.e "yourname.wordpress.com"), while the software with the pro features and support is available at Wordpress.org. From that site you can download the software (it's free) so that Wordpress can be installed on your web host (most web hosting platforms already have it installed these days). Doing this will allow your blog to use your personal URL (i.e. "yourname.com").

Figure 11.2: The Wordpress post entry page

One reason that many pros choose Wordpress is that even though Blogger is owned by Google, Wordpress blogs seem to consistently rank higher in Google search rankings. I've seen this for myself, as when I switch over to a Wordpress blog my views went up by 20%!

While using the services of Wordpress.com's blog hosting is about as easy as using Blogger, setting one up from scratch using the hosted Wordpress software can be tricky. Although there are plenty of design templates (themes, as they're called) that you can buy that seem like they're an out-of-the-box solution, that's usually not the case, so be prepared to spend some time learning how to make things look and perform the way you want. There are plenty of good tutorials that can be found on YouTube and the web, but I've found the ones on Lynda.com to be particularly good. You can go to lynda.com/trial/bowsinski for a free seven day trial.

TIP: Be careful when buying a Wordpress theme since the features you may want may be available only in the "Pro" version of the package, which can cost considerably more than you expect to spend.

Regardless of which version of Wordpress that you use, the price is right, as in free. That's not to say that it's cost-free however, since getting the exact look and features you want will cost you either in time, the cost of a template, or hiring the help you need to make it work.

Typepad

Typepad (see Figure 11.3) is more of a business platform in that it's very easy to add monetization modules, it has a great user interface, and its look can be programmed from the ground up. The down side is that it will cost you anywhere from $8.95 to $29.95 per month for the privilege of using the platform, as well as having to pay for the services of someone to program it for you if needed. That said, Typepad has amazing support from real live people, while the other platforms basically rely on forums to answer your questions.

Figure 11.3: Typepad post entry page

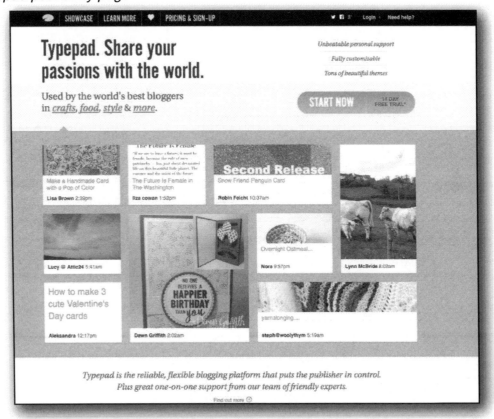

If you're new to blogging, you're much better off starting with either Blogger or Wordpress to get your feet wet before transitioning to Typepad. This is for pros only.

Medium

Medium was founded in 2012 by Ev Williams, the co-founder of both Twitter and Blogger, so much of the way it works come's from his previous experiences. It's different from other blog platforms in that it's less of a personalized blogging platform and more of a community-centric writing tool. In other words, writing on Medium is like publishing your article in the magazine or the notice-board rather than in a journal or diary of your own (see Figure 11.4).

Figure 11.4: Medium home page

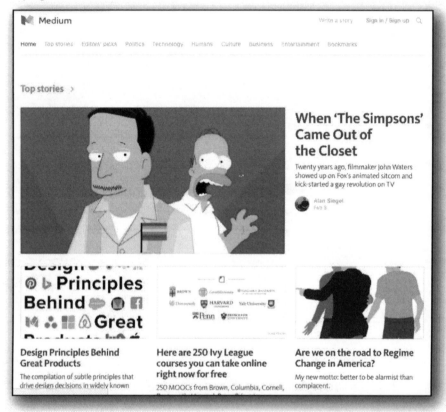

Medium is purely a hosted platform, so you can't run it on your own server. It looks really really good on almost any device, although there's not much to customize in terms of design. There are no storage limits, and it's totally free as of now, which includes custom domains, sub-domains, SSL, and everything else that's an extra charge on other platforms.

The downside is that since your blog is hosted by Medium, the audience isn't really yours and you may lose them after they finish reading your post. You're competing with other authors/writers so your posts need to stand out right from the beginning. Plus, you don't have full control around the user experience, which may compromise your brand.

Tumblr

Tumblr is perhaps the fastest and easiest to set up, but that's at the expense of looks and features (see Figure 11.5). Actually, Tumblr is more accurately defined as a microblogging site because it straddles the boundary between a blog or a social media site. That means that the posts are shorter and actively encourage personal communication with the reader.

Figure 11.5: Tumblr home page

While Tumblr is widely used, it has far fewer features than any of the other platforms. What Tumblr really is good at is that it's very personal and intimate, and if you want a younger audience, this is a good way to get it since they've embraced the platform with vigor. That can also be a downside as well, but it all depends upon the demographic of the fans you're trying to reach.

A big turn-of for many prospective bloggers is that Tumblr blogs look and feel the same, even though you can skin them differently in the same way that your Twitter page can be customized. You also don't have the advantage of widgets, but what you do have is quick and instant communication.

What's interesting is that many pro bloggers host their professional blog on one of the other platforms, yet keep a personal one on Tumblr because it provides the most intimate of all blog engagement.

Which To Choose?

If your website package has a blogging feature and isn't too much trouble to set up, that's the way to go to keep people on your site. If you just want to get a blog up and running as quickly as possible yet still have the ability to control the design and features somewhat, I'd opt for Blogger. That said, choose the one that you feel most comfortable with. You can always change to a different platform later down the road.

Blog Design

While continuity between your website and social media is important, your blog is one place where the content is truly king. As a result, it's better to get started blogging immediately using a plain vanilla template than to wait until you create the perfect design. Because of the way blog platforms are implemented, your custom design can be inserted at just about any time. That said, you still do want to brand it so it's consistent with the rest of your online presence.

Even with their most basic templates, most blog platforms and themes give you a wide variety of looks and functionality to choose from. Among the things you can modify are the appearance of:

- The blog header
- The navigation bar
- The layout of the page
- The color of the text on the header, sidebar or posts
- How many posts appear on the page
- If the entire post will be viewed or only a portion
- The background color of both the header, the page, and behind the text
- Insertion of widgets (limited function apps within the page)
- A blog roll (links to suggested blog)
- Your blog archives
- Your other websites or those that you recommend

These are just the tip of the iceberg, as you'll find a host of different features that you can customize with each template (see Figure 11.6).

Figure 11.6: The Blogger layout page

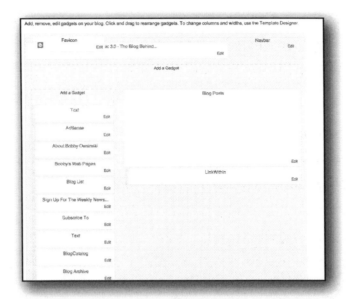

The design of your blog isn't critical for it to be a success, but it does help your branding if it's consistent with your website and social media presence. That said, it's better to have a blog presence immediately than to wait until you get the design just right. It's easy enough to tweak the design later as you go along. Let's look at the major elements that go into designing your blog.

The Template Or Theme

After you register for the platform, the first thing you'll have to do when setting up your blog is to choose a template, or if you're in Wordpress, the theme. This can take a lot longer than you think, as most platforms have dozens to choose from, as well as many variations on each. Plus, each can be modified in terms of style, color and placement of the elements. Most likely you won't find exactly what you're looking for, but choose something that's close and modify it as needed.

Those modifications can be quick and easy or can be down to the html and CSS level if you have the chops. In order to get started, just get something that puts you in the ballpark first.

Layout

The layout consists of the elements that you'll be using and where they're placed on the page. On some platforms, this is easier than on others, but once again, try to get it in the ballpark just so you can get started.

Header

The header contains the name of your blog, logo graphic (if you have one), contact info (if you choose to list it) and sometimes menu items. Especially give the some thought as it may stay with you for a long time. Also remember that it's best if your name or the name of your band is involved, if not in the header name, than in a subtitle.

Profile

Finally, be sure to set up a profile or "About" page. Make sure you have a real current picture, not one of an avatar or when you were a kid. People that read blogs want to relate to the author, and they can't do that if you don't feel comfortable enough to show them who you are.

Your RSS Feed

RSS stands for Really Simple Syndication and allows people to easily stay informed by automatically retrieving the latest content from the sites they're interested in. These posts are read through what's known as an RSS reader, which can be either a stand-alone app or built into your browser. This saves time by not needing to visit each blog individually or joining each blog's email newsletter, and allows the reader to review a large amount of information in a short amount of time. For a publisher (that's you, the blog owner), feeds permit instant distribution of content with the ability to make it "subscribable." RSS feeds use a universal icon as seen in Figure 11.7.

Figure 11.7: The universal RSS feed icon

Most modern web browsers handle RSS feeds, but in a limited manner. They use an RSS feed as a dynamic bookmark folder with automatic bookmarks to all the news in the feed. Unlike news aggregators, browsers will not save the news if you don't check on it every day.

Even though RSS has been the standard for web feeds for a long time now, it's often confusing and uses non-standard conventions due to its scattered development over time. As a result, a newer syndication standard called ATOM was created in response to the design flaws of RSS. Essentially both RSS and ATOM do the same thing, but ATOM does it better and is designed to be somewhat future-proof. If you have a choice of which standard to use, choose ATOM, but don't lose any sleep over it if that choice is not available.

RSS feed URLs look something like this:

Atom: http://blogname.blogspot.com/feeds/posts/default
RSS: http://blogname.blogspot.com/feeds/posts/default?alt=rss

In this case, we're looking at feeds from the Blogger platform, but substitute "wordpress" for "blogspot" and it looks the same for that platform (see Figure 11.8).

Figure 11.8: The RSS feed from Blogger

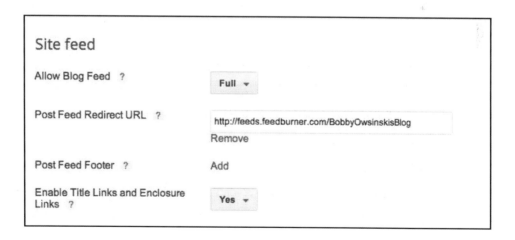

FeedBurner

Google Feedburner is a feed management service that makes your blog feed easy to subscribe to. Once you sign in from your Google account, you claim your feed by simply typing in your blog address. In most cases, Feedburner automatically extracts the feed address from your blog (see Figure 11.9).

Figure 11.9: The Feedburner feed extraction or "burn" page

You can then add buttons to your site, like a subscriber button, a generic RSS button, or choose from dozens of others such as ones for Google Reader, Netvibes, Bloglines, etc. Just pick the button you want, your blogging platform, and Feedburner provides the HTML code. It's been found that readers are more likely to subscribe if you offer a button for the newsreader they're already using and familiar with, so it helps to give your readers a few options here.

Since Feedburner is a feed management system, it allows you to consolidate multiple feeds into one. This can make it easier for your readers to consume multiple blogs (if you have them) and for you to measure what they're reading. Speaking of which, Feedburner also has a range of analytics available that looks at your subscribers and what they consume and react to.

Feedblitz

Not everyone understands RSS and Atom feeds, and only a fraction of Internet users know what these are and how use them. If you don't provide an alternative mechanism for users to subscribe to your content, you're missing out on reaching over 80% of your potential audience.

A very convenient service that aggregates your posts and sends them to your followers in an email is Feedblitz. Since many people don't want the hassle or complexity of dealing with a feed subscription, receiving these posts by email works perfectly well for them, and that's what Feedblitz does. It puts a subscription box on your blog where people can sign up to get an email with all your posts from the previous day or week.

Feedblitz handles the post summaries for nearly 100,000 blogs and allows for a pretty good level of interactivity and analytics. It watches over your email list the same as the email services described in Chapter 5, allows you to set when the email is sent and what's in it, and handles multiple sites (see Figure 11.10). While all this used to be free, now the prices are similar to other email services in that they're based on the number of active subscribers on the list.

Figure 11.10: The Feedblitz dashboard

The fact is, if you already have a mailing list provider, you can probably arrange for it to do the same thing as Feedblitz. Just check that it will accept an RSS feed and you're good to go. If not, give Feedblitz a try at feedbiltz.com.

TIP: It's always better if you can keep all your lists together with the same email list provider (that's why I switched from Feedblitz to GetResponse to send my blog digests out).

What To Write About

Just creating a blog for the sake of having a blog probably isn't a good idea. You want to be doing it because you have more to say than can be properly handled by your social media platforms. If you're an expert in a subject, that should be pretty easy because you probably have a lot of ideas regarding the current state of your business, it's future, and the topics of the day. If you're a musician, you probably have plenty to blog about as well. Typical topics might be about:

- **Life on the road.** A look at the various towns, venues and the people you meet while traveling from town to town.

- **Life in the studio**. Behind the scenes in the studio, the personnel you're working with (the studio manager, the engineer, assistant, etc.), how a song was written and developed, what kind of instruments or mics you used, how long it took to record and mix, and a million other things that so many fans find interesting.

- **Life in the business.** The music business continues to evolve and you probably have lots of thoughts on piracy, streaming, ticketing, 360 deals, record labels, management and everything else that goes on behind the scenes.

- **Life outside the business.** Maybe you're a runner, a vegan, a skydiver or a baseball fan, and you want to discuss these issues separately from your music.

- **Topics of the day.** Maybe you're politically charged. If so, follow a site like Politico (or Fox News on television) and give your take on some of their articles or commentaries. If something like GreenTech is your thing, then set up a Google Alert for every time that's mentioned in the news in order to keep your readers up on the latest advances (see the next section for more details).

As I mentioned previously, I write two blogs five days a week and that means I always have to have something to say, even when I think I have nothing. Here are some tricks I use:

- **Post a video.** Go to YouTube and find a video that you think your readers might like. Embed it into your blog (click *Share* below the video, then *Embed*, copy the code and paste it into the html of your blog), then write a brief take on what you liked or didn't like, or about some of the special things to notice when watching.

- **Follow some newsmakers on Twitter or Facebook.** Perhaps there's a site you really like that constantly has posts and articles that might be relevant to your blog. Follow them on social media (or just read them every day), then either use their topics for ideas to write about, or quote a portion of an article in your post.

TIP: *Don't directly copy an article and use it as your own. It's misleading, dishonest and a form of piracy. If you do copy something or use a portion, be sure to provide a link back to the original post and give profuse attribution to both the site and the author.*

- **Keep a list of topics handy.** Whenever I see something that I think might be useful to my readers, I immediately copy the link and create a quick draft post that isn't published, but I can come back to at a later time. That way, I always have about ten topics that I can refer to if one day I come up dry, or I know I'll be traveling or in the studio and won't have time to create something new.

- **Create a Google Alert.** A Google Alert is a short post that Google will send you whenever a certain topic is posted. For instance, I have one for all of my books, so if someone posts about *Music 3.0*, I get an alert with a link to where it was posted. That way I can follow the link and read the post or article for myself. You can do the same thing with any topic. If your passion is Tibet, you can create a Google Alert for any articles and posts on Tibet. If that's too broad, you can narrow it to "horse racing in Tibet" (be sure to use the quotes to tell Google to use the entire phrase) and just receive alerts whenever something on that topic is posted. Go to google.com/alerts to create and keep track of alerts.

- **Once a month, do a search.** Take a period of time every month (I take about 30 minutes) and do a search about a particular topic. Believe me, you'll have so many links to choose from with so many points of view that you can't but help get ideas for a few posts.

- **Make a list.** People love lists because they're easy to consume. Top ten lists are always good (it could be either your top 10 or someone else's), checklists are fun, and "xx (pick a number) best tips" are always good. It doesn't matter how many items are on the list, just that you've made one.

- **Interview someone.** Even if you've run out of things to say, chances are you know someone who has plenty to contribute. Simply interview a friend or colleague for new post material. I used to have a weekly post I called "6 Questions," where I asked the same six questions to a different person every week. The trick here is to have enough questions that you still have something interesting if someone doesn't write too well or feel like writing at all, but not so many as to make it seem like work. Of course, you can always do a live audio or video interview, or do Facebook or YouTube Live, then post the result on your blog. The point is, don't limit your posts to just you.

- **Guest Posts.** Speaking of having another voice, you can always open up your blog for a guest post either from a friend, band member, or even an avid reader who posts a lot of comments.

- **Post an excerpt.** I'm an author so it's easy for me to post a short excerpt from a chapter in one of my books, but if you want to write your first book, here's where to start. Begin by posting bits and pieces of your upcoming chapters. If you've written some magazine articles or reviews, you can repost a part or all of them (make sure you get permission if you don't own them yourself).

- **Repost a favorite.** After you've been blogging for a while, hopefully you'll find that your audience is increasing. That means that your new readers probably haven't seen any of your earlier posts unless they've gone back and read all your archives (which most probably haven't done). It's okay to post something that you've previously posted, as long as there's been enough time since it was last posted. I like to let at least a year go by. Make sure that you identify it as a previous post.

That's just a few ideas for posting if you go dry. Remember, there's always something to write about if you look around hard enough.

Post Length

Some people get into long, rambling posts that go on for several thousand words. Keep in mind that most readers probably won't stand for that on a regular basis. They don't have that kind of time to spend, and if you've done that amount of work without the help of an editor, chances are you could have said the same thing with more impact in about half as many words.

That's why it's best if you keep each post to between 300 to 900 words, especially if you post frequently. These are very digestible bites, and even if a reader doesn't necessarily like the particular post, they don't feel like they've wasted much time after reading it. If you only post monthly or even quarterly (not a good idea, as you'll see), then you can get away with a much longer post, since each one is almost like its own event.

My Writing Method

When I write my books (including this one) I use what I call "The Three Pass Method." That means that in the case of a book, each chapter gets at least three writing passes. I've found this to be so successful that I use the same method for writing everything, as well as for other types of creation as well. Here's how it works.

Pass 1: Stream of consciousness. The first pass is totally stream of consciousness where I don't worry about spelling, punctuation, grammar or anything else. All I want to do is get the ideas on the paper (figuratively speaking, since I'm using a computer) before I forget them. You are not looking for, nor care about, perfection.

Pass 2: Refinement. The second pass is refinement, where I go through and fix all the things that I let slide during the first pass. This is where I pound sentences into understandable paragraphs, insert the correct punctuation, and fix all the spelling errors.

Pass 3: Polishing. The third pass is polishing, and this is where I go through the entire chapter after everything's been fixed and do any final tweaks that the text might need. Usually at this point you can notice if a sentence doesn't make as much sense as you originally intended, or if you're failing to get your point across in a paragraph.

Sometimes I may go through a fourth or fifth time as well, but never more than five, because by that time, I'm just making things different and not necessarily better. Each of these passes are on a different day to make sure that I have enough time to get away from the project and clear my head to get a fresher perspective on things.

Applying The Method To A Blog

I use a condensed version of this method for writing my blogs, since I don't have the time to wait three days for three different passes. It's not as effective as my book-oriented three day method, as some errors occasionally slip through, but it's surprisingly efficient.

What I do is write my first pass in a stream of conscious manner to just get the ideas down, then I immediately do a second pass to tighten things up. I always post a photo with every blog, so the time I spend looking for something appropriate is enough time for me to get away from the blog to look at it with a somewhat fresh eye when I come back to insert the photo in the post. At this time, I do one last pass to make sure everything looks okay and tweak wherever it's needed. I may make a fourth pass later in the day if I feel that I didn't get something right or some new information presents itself, but that doesn't happen often.

All told, each post takes me from 15 minutes to an hour to create, depending upon the complexity (really complex ones like my song analysis posts can take longer). That said, the time is about half of what it was when I first started blogging, and the same will happen to you as well. Experience will make your posting faster.

Photos In Posts

Just like on Facebook or Twitter, a photo inserted into a blog post can result in an increased number of views. This doesn't have to be a recent photo or even one that you took yourself, it just has to relate to the post. Of course, a graphic designed in Photoshop or another graphic design program can have the same effect as a photo.

If you're tempted to do a Google graphic search and use a photo off the web, keep in mind that if you use a picture without permission, somewhere down the road you may be asked to either pay a fee or delete it from your site.

There are a number of sites that provide royalty-free images with no or low-restrictions, like FreeRangeStock, Pixabay, Unsplash, Photodropper, and 500px.

LinkWithin

A very cool blog widget that shows and links related stories under each post is called LinkWithin. The widget retrieves and indexes all stories from your blog archive, not just recent stories, making them accessible to new or casual readers of your blog who would not otherwise encounter them. The widget links to stories that are relevant and interesting to readers of a particular post, keeping them engaged with your blog, and increasing your traffic (see Figure 11.11).

Figure 11.11: LinkWithin recommendations

The best part is the widget is free and also ad-free. It's available for Blogger, Wordpress (self-hosted) and Typepad, but a version can also be installed on other blog platforms as well. The LinkWithin site makes it easy to install into your blog, and provides instructions to make it appear right below your blog post. It takes about the same amount of time to install it as it took you to read about about it. This widget is well-worth installing since it provides valuable backlinks to your past material.

The Secrets To A Successful Blog

I've been blogging for almost 10 years now, going from a grand total of five views the first week on my production blog, to well over 120,000 a month as I write this (the *Music 3.0 blog* is at about 60,000). I blog every weekday (five days a week) every week with no breaks for holidays or vacations. Every morning at 9AM Eastern you'll see my latest post, which as you'll see, is one of the secrets to a successful blog. Let's have a look at all of the secrets:

1. Post on a consistent basis. This is the number one most important rule of blogging. Once you decide you're going to blog, your next decision is when and how often you're going to do it. Once that's decided, it's best if you stick with that forever! If you decide that you're going to blog every Tuesday at noon, then you better be sure that next Tuesday at noon a new mussing will be posted no matter what. This is actually pretty easy in that all blog platforms now have a built-in scheduler so you can write your post whenever you're inspired, then have it post at your designated time. In fact, as I write this I'm sitting on the promenade deck of a cruise ship anchored off an island in the Bahamas. I knew I'd have a spotty, expensive Internet connection this week, so I wrote an entire week of blog posts in advance that will post at exactly 9AM every morning while I'm away.

You may ask why I chose 9AM as the my time to post and I'll tell you that when I first started blogging, the time when I generally finished writing my posts was at 9:30PM. Since I had inadvertently chosen a blogging time, I knew I had to stick with it, so posted at 9:30PM for a number of years, even though I generally write each post early in the morning.

But posting anything after 9PM at night is not a great idea if you want to reach the most people, so I eventually changed to 9AM EST even though I almost always write my posts the day before. If there's some breaking news that I want to post about, I'll just reschedule my original post for another day, and I still have time to write the new post while the content is still relevant.

Why do you need to be consistent? Studies have shown that by losing your consistency, you begin to suffer viewer attrition. If people can't be sure when you'll post, they generally don't check in as often. Think of your favorite television program. If you know that it will be shown every Tuesday night at 8PM, you set your schedule around that (forgetting for a minute that you can also might be able to watch it on YouTube or Netflix afterwards). If the network begins to change the time of broadcast (or even worse, the day), then you don't know when to tune in and find something else to watch at that time instead. Same with your blog.

2. The more frequently you post, the better. The way to get regular viewers is to have frequent posts. More posts give you more of a chance to get more readers. I'm not suggesting that you should post every day like I do (that's a hard schedule, believe me), but once a month isn't enough to get any traction either. That said, you have to have something to write about as well, so be sure you have plenty of material to fill up those posts. Once or twice a week is plenty in most cases.

TIP: *The less frequently you post, the longer the posts should be. 300 words per post works okay for once a day, but 700 to 900 is better for once a week.*

---

3. Content is king. When it's all said and done, a blog is successful because the content was useful to the reader. It doesn't matter where it came from, if the reader feels that his time was well-spent on your blog, then you'll be successful. That doesn't mean that every post has to be a home run, but you have to have a high batting average, and you will if you take blogging seriously.

Why Blogs Fail

There are five main reasons why blogs never get any traction or can't keep readers after they get them. They are:

1. Inconsistent posting. Assuming that you have something to say, a knack for saying it, and people who want to hear it, the biggest reason why a blog fails is because it's not updated on a consistent enough basis. The more you post, the more likely your blog will find followers. The more consistently you post, the more regularly they'll read.

2. Non-relevant posts. All good blogs have a theme. It can be narrow (my music production blog is about strictly about music creation and production while my *Music 3.0 blog* is about the music industry) or it could be wide (your daily life, like my friend Quinn Cummings' ever entertaining QC Report), but the fact is that the readers come to your blog expecting a consistent theme. If your posts are suddenly off-topic (say local politics on a hi-fi blog), that's when you see the most reader attrition occur. For a wide-themed blog, that could mean getting too specific too much of the time (post after post about dogs, for example). Find your theme, then stay on-topic as much as you can.

3. Posts that say nothing. Many bloggers get into trouble by posting what amounts to a bunch of words with no point, or posts that add no new information for the reader. Every reader is short on time, and if he feels robbed of that time from reading a post that adds nothing to his life, he may soon become an ex-reader. Have a take, be provocative, or provide a different perception or point of view; anything to make the reader feel that the minutes it took to read your blog were well-spent.

4. Posts that are too negative. Unless your blog is based on something negative (like "the end of the world is coming"), blog posts that are consistently negative turn readers off. It's okay to go negative sometimes, and it's even good for a blog to have some controversy, but post after negative post will usually lose far more readers than it adds.

5. Posts that fan the flame wars. Flame wars are running battles with commenters. Someone will make a comment that takes issue with something you posted, and you take issue back, which leads to the commenter taking issue with your taking issue, and you taking issue back yet again. This goes back and forth and usually changes the subject several times (getting more personal as it goes along) as it descends into something that most readers don't want to follow. Where you really can get into trouble is posting about a negative comment, as that just stokes the war even more. After a few rounds of this, sane viewers run away.

TIP: The best way to stop a flame war from starting is to refuse to respond to a negative comment. If you feel compelled to respond, just make a single comment as an answer and don't engage again.

Blog SEO

Search Engine Optimization applies to blog posts the same way it applies to your website. While a good user experience and great content are still the key to SEO, being aware of a few things can make a difference if someone is searching for you on Google or any of the other search engines (there are well over 100 believe it or not).

- **The post title:** Ideally you want a title that's short and easy to spell with a keyword in it. Preferably the keyword would be the first word, if possible. That may make for a title that reads badly, but I wouldn't obsess over it, just be aware. The best keyword is one that's both relative to, and can be found in the post.

- **The post slug:** The slug is the URL of the post. For instance, http://music3point0.com/2017/07/31/radio-pennsylvania/ is an example of a slug for a post from my Music 3.0 blog called "Radio Faces A Big Test In Pennsylvania That Will Affect The Country." It usually contains the date of the post, as well well as something to describe what the post is about. The key here is to make sure that if there's a keyword that you're using in the title, make sure that it's also in the slug as well. In this case there are two keywords, "radio" and "Pennsylvania."

- **The post body:** Once again, the strongest SEO is when one of the keywords appears in the first paragraph, then between one and two percent of the text. That means that if your keyword phrase is "recording studio" for example, it should appear once or twice per hundred words. If it doesn't, don't worry as your ranking won't drop a huge amount just because of that, but if helps a bit if you remember the rule.

- **The post graphics:** Every picture or graphic should have an "alt" title, which is an alternate title that appears if a browser can't interpret your page and just shows text (see Figure 11.12). As it turns out, search engines love these tags, so make sure that you fill them in, and make sure they have the exact same keywords as the title text.

Figure 11.12: An Alt title

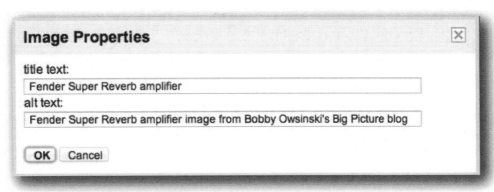

- **The meta tags:** Meta tags are keywords that describe your post. All blogging platforms have the ability to insert these with a post. Not only are they helpful for SEO purposes, but they're useful when doing a search of your archives as well.

TIP: If you're using Wordpress for your blog, an excellent plugin is Yoast SEO, which will guide you to creating an SEO-optimized post.

Using Topic Clusters As A Content Strategy

Through the years Google and other search engines have gotten a lot smarter, and the way we use them has changed as a result. In the past, if we wanted to search for a guitar repair shop, we'd usually have to know the name of the shop we were looking for first, like "World Guitar Repair." Now we can type in something like "Where can I get a guitar repaired" and Google is smart enough to know our intent and give us a more targeted result with more usable choices. That's why our content strategy on websites, blogs and YouTube channels must change in order to take advantage of how Google currently works, and the latest idea is something called Topic Clusters.

The old way of thinking about SEO (search engine optimization) was that it was based around keywords, but after so many people tried to game the system by inserting dozens or even hundreds of keywords at every opportunity, Google began to give them less importance to the point where they mean very little these days. Topic clusters have replaced keywords instead, and they make a lot more sense for today's online content world.

In a topic cluster, there's one long post or video that broadly outlines a topic (called the "pillar post"), then shorter "cluster" posts (or videos) each about a different detail of the pillar topic with a link back to the pillar. In order to be most effective, the pillar post should also link back to the cluster posts. If one of the cluster posts does well, then they all get a boost (see Figure 11.13).

What happens is that Google's webcrawlers notice the semantic relationship between all the topics and gives you a boost in its search engine results. it also makes it easier for your readers or viewers to find and consume your information as well.

Figure 11.13: Topic clusters

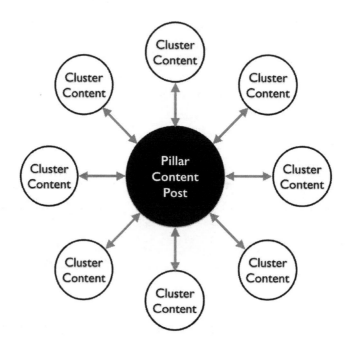

Promoting Your Blog

The beauty of a blog is that it works in synergy with all your other social media because there's an element of cross-promotion involved. That means that you can promote your blog on your social media (as well as your website), and promote your social media on your blog.

One of the things that I do is post to both Twitter and Facebook about what I post on my blog. I'll post or tweet the title of the blog post as well as a short description of what the post is about. That way more people are aware of the blog post in general, and the topic in particular if it interests them. Here's an example:

The Band Pre-Production Checklist. Tips to make your band record-ready. bit.ly/1s5safC #recording #musicians

Take notice there's a link to the blog, as well as the appropriate hashtags for Twitter. Since the lifespan of a tweet is so short, I usually just insert the blog link instead the individual post link where it shows up on its own page. If I ever repost something from the archive, then I'll use the individual post link.

I'll also be sure to post Facebook and Twitter links on the blog so people can follow me if they like.

Popular Blog List Sites

One way to get your blog noticed is to submit it to some of the popular blog list sites. These are also a great way to find blogs to follow as well. Here's a brief list of the top sites:

- **Alltop**: Perhaps the grandfather of all blog discovery sites, Alltop is known for its tight topic-based groupings.

- **BlogCatalog**: A good looking site that regularly features niche blogs that are frequently overlooked on other blog directories.

- **BlogSearchEngine**: This is directory that allows you to look for topics that you're interested in.

- **Spillbean Blog Directory**: Once again, this is a topic-based directory, but it has the distinct advantage of having specific categories you can search under.

- **Blogging Fusion**: This site is also searchable with categories but also has a list of the top blogs and tags.

All of these sites have a submission area where you can submit your blog to be listed in their directory. It doesn't take long (although it may take a few days before the listing becomes active) and can be well worth it when it comes to gaining followers.

Tying Your Blog To Your Website

Regardless if it's your website, blog, Facebook page or YouTube channel, people come back more regularly if there's new material posted. Because it takes longer to redesign a website than almost anything else online, site owners usually do it a lot less often than they should, but the one way to keep your site refreshed with new material is to tie your blog to it.

This can be done a couple of ways. For instance, you can use the blog's RSS feed to link to a section of your site (see Figure 11.14). The problem with this is that even though your visitors will notice, Google might not, which negates some of the effect of the refreshed content.

Figure 11.14: Using the RSS feed to display my blogs on a website home page

The other way is have the blog be a part of the home page of your site, with links to the rest of your site. In this case, the blog would have the same domain name as your site (in my case, bobbyowsinski.com). Of course, if Wordpress has already been installed on your hosting site, this can be a little easier to implement. Either way, your site will be refreshed with new material, which will keep viewers returning.

Using A Blogging Platform As A Website

Many web designers have learned that a blogging platform (especially Wordpress) can make a wonderful platform for a website. Blogs originally featured a single page with posts, but through the years they've developed the ability to have multiple pages complete with links from a main page. Now many platforms and templates have become so sophisticated that most of the features of web design software like Adobe Dreamweaver are actually built directly into the blogging platform. These include drop-down menus, rotating banners, tabbed and toggled content, SEO control, and much more.

While using a blogging platform like Wordpress can provide a very quick modern looking website, the reason why many designers like it is because it's also fairly easy for an end user to update when they're ready. The downside is that while a web design app basically gives you a "what you see is what you get" picture of your site before it's published, using a blog platform for a website basically means that you may be designing off-line in the abstract, and only see how it really looks when you publish it (see Figure 11.15). This can take a fair amount of time for a beginner to get the hang of, as it takes some experience to get a feel for what will happen before you actually tell it to do so. A quick way to learn how to program Wordpress to act as a website is through one of the Lynda.com Wordpress courses. Go to lynda.com/trial/bowsinski for a free trial.

TIP: *A number of Wordpress themes now feature a visual interface, although most with this feature are not free.*

Figure 11.15: The appearance panel for the Luxe Wordpress theme

Making Money With Your Blog

Yes, it is possible to actually make money from your blog if you have sufficient readership. To do this, you must decide that it's okay to go commercial and it won't be a hinderance to your audience's enjoyment, since it will require some ads to be inserted onto the page. Here are the two main ways that revenue is generated from a blog.

Google Adsense

Google AdSense is a program that allows blog and website owners to host automatic media adverts that are targeted to the site content and audience. These adverts are administered, sorted, and maintained by Google, and they generate revenue on either a per-click or per-impression basis.

You actually have quite a bit of control over Adsense adverts in that you can control the number of ads per page, how large they are, and where they're located (see Figure 11.16). Although Google figures out the general audience that would work best for your content after a few days, you always maintain the ability to block or filter certain ads, advertisers, or certain categories of ads.

Figure 11.16: A Google ad in the sidebar on my Music 3.0 blog

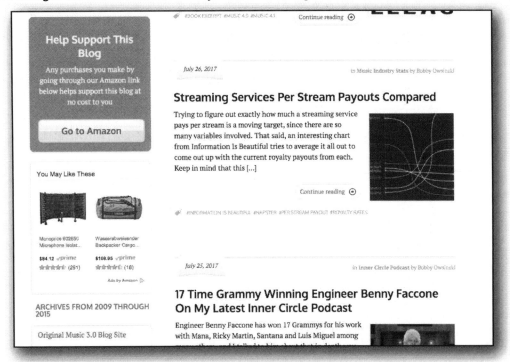

Most bloggers are apprehensive of inserting ads after they've built their following, but it generally has little effect on readership if done in moderation, since most visitors are already used to seeing ads on other web and blog pages. I've found that an ad on the sidebar and another after every second post works well without seeming intrusive.

To sign up for Adsense, go to google.com/adsense. You'll need an existing Google account (which most likely you already have if you have a Gmail account), but you can also use a new Google account as well. After you've registered, you select the sites or blogs that you'd like to monetize, then provide either banking information so Google can directly deposit into your checking or savings account, or a snail mail address so they can send you a check. Google Adsense also provides a nice set of analytics that show how much you make daily and from what source.

Another benefit from Adsense is that you can also set it to insert ads in your RSS feeds and on your YouTube videos (more on that in Chapter 9 about YouTube).

Affiliate Programs

Another way to make money is to be a part of an affiliate program from Amazon, Rakuten, or others. With an affiliate program, a link is placed in the text that takes the reader directly to the product page for more information or a purchase. If a product is purchased, you receive a royalty payment. The more purchases that are made through your site in a month, the more your royalty rate increases.

The best part of affiliate links is that a person doesn't have to purchase only the item that was linked in your blog. Once the reader arrives on the seller's site, any purchase from that point on is credited to you.

I always put affiliate links in a blog post if it's pertinent, especially when one of my books is mentioned. The interesting thing is that each month my books are only between one-third to one-half of the purchases that I receive a royalty on. Considering that both of my blogs pertain to music, I've received royalties on baby carriages, women's apparel, tools, and a host of other decidedly non-music purchases.

Amazon is pretty much a can't-miss affiliate in that it sells such a wide variety of items (see Figure 11.17). To register, go to affiliate-program.amazon.com. The registration procedure is similar to Google Adsense. For Rakuten (which is the largest affiliate program other than Amazon), go to rakutenmarketing.com. The good thing about Rakuten is that it represents a wide range of businesses, from Macy's to Wine USA to Tiger Direct to Hotels.com and hundreds more. It's also the easiest way to become an iTunes affiliate.

Figure 11.17: The Amazon Affiliate window

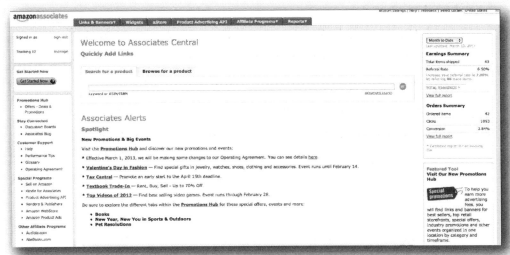

Blogging can not only be one of the most rewarding and fulfilling activities that you can do online, but it can also be a powerful item in your promotional toolbox as well. It's virtually free and easy to set up, and can truly provide a host of benefits if you're willing to follow the recommendations outlined in this chapter.

12

Playlist Marketing

While radio airplay used to be the lifeblood of a hit (and in some cases still is), today it's the streaming service playlist that really sets the tone for listener discovery.

If a track is added to a popular playlist, its streams will spike and listeners will add it to their personal playlists, which sometimes adds a viral element that spreads to playlists on other networks as well. What's more, hot playlists are now watched by radio programmers to see both what's trending and what's not.

The problem is that while the playlist culture has been great for music discovery for the listener, it turns out it hasn't been that great for artist development. Where before listeners were getting to know the artist's music via multiple songs on an album, that's all changed as streaming has made the business more song-driven instead of artist-driven.

As a result, songs tend to come and go faster, as do artists. The good news is that means there are are always some spots open on a playlist for new songs. The bad news is that it's more difficult for an artist to get long-term traction.

Getting Your Music On Popular Playlists

Spotify and Apple Music playlists are getting harder and harder to crack, especially if you're not on a major label. Here are a few tips that can land you a spot on a playlist from Spotify or any other playlist.

1. Verify your profiles with Spotify and Apple Connect. The first thing you have to do is make sure you have a presence on the service itself. Playlist curators, especially if they're in-house, are reluctant to feature anything by artists who've not verified their profiles on the streaming platforms.

To verify your Spotify account you must first submit your account for verification. This requires:

- Your Spotify URL link

- Your Spotify personal username

- Your artist profile name

- Your Twitter account

2. Get as many of your fans as possible to follow you on the streaming platform. You don't need millions of followers or streams, but you don't need enough to get a curator interested. They want to know that you have a buzz around you before they take a chance. Who to follow? How about:

- Music bloggers and music news websites

- Magazines and weeklies

- Political figures

- Authors and poets

- Radio stations

- Other bands and artists

- Brands

- Music fans

- Spotify curators (or the curators on the service or your choice)

- And finally, your own playlist (you do have one, don't you?)

3. Get the rest of your digital house in order. If a curator is interested in your music, he or she will probably check you out further by looking at your website, photos, social media, upcoming gigs and all the things that we've talking about in this book. Here's where that all comes into play.

4. Find some playlists to follow. Find some playlists that you love and begin to follow them with the idea of learning if your music is a fit. Don't limit yourself to Spotify's in-house curators. In this game, they all count because the idea is to ultimately get on a number of smaller playlists first so you'll be noticed by the Spotify team. Also make sure to follow them on social media, and make comments where and when you can.

5. Make your pitch. Make sure that the playlist owner is well aware of you before you begin your pitch. You'll be taken much more seriously if you're recognized as a supporter rather than someone just cold-calling. Send a personally crafted email to the playlist owner or curator. Make it brief and to the point and tell them why you think your song is perfect for their list. Be as specific as you can and avoid being long-winded. If a curator has a submission policy, make sure that you follow it to the letter or chances are your submission won't even be read.

Remember that some curators for the larger lists make their selections in a closed system, so they don't want pitches and they'll usually make that clear in their submission policy. If that's the case, respect their wishes and don't hassle them. The only way you're going to get to them is if you begin to get on a lot of other playlists so your buzz will be noticed.

Playlist Promotion

Not surprisingly, pay-to-play has come to the digital age as a new form of payola now attempts to influence what consumers listen to. Playlist promotion, or "playola," has become a big part of the promotional campaigns for many managers and labels.

Prices for playlist promotion can be as little as $100 to a small blogger with a modest following, to as much as $10,000 for a six-week campaign for a major playlist owner. A quick Google search will turn up dozens of promotion companies that specialize in getting your songs on playlists everywhere.

Just like in the old days of radio promotion, competition is now fierce for these playlist spots, so don't be surprised if the prices continue to rise.

Submitting Your Music To Streaming Services

Most online music streaming services, especially Spotify and Apple Music, no longer take submissions from individual artists or even small indie record labels. It's possible to easily get your music on all of these services but you need to go through an aggregator like TuneCore, CD Baby, Distrokid, or Reverbnation.

If you have an indie label, another way would be to register with MerlinNetwork.org, the independent label association. Merlin represents by far the most commercially significant set of rights outside of the three major labels with 800+ members representing tens of thousands of labels from 53 countries that accounts for more than 12% of the global market. Merlin negotiates deals with all online distributors using the power of its large membership. The organization provides tools to submit your music to all the streaming services.

Treating Spotify Like A Social Platform

Many musicians are adept in at least one of the major social media platforms (Facebook, Instagram, Twitter), but aren't aware that those skills are transferrable to a platform that requires a lot more social interaction that you might think, and that's Spotify. The service has done a good job not only as a music distributor, but has installed some usable social features around it as well. This is one of the things that sets it apart from other streaming services. Granted, others have tried (hello Apple Music), but haven't been able to pull off the social aspect with as much impact on the both the user and the artist.

That said, this excerpt from an excellent article on CD Baby's DIY Musician blog outlines the steps that you can take to amplify the social aspects of Spotify. Here they are, with my comments afterwards:

1. Update your playlists with new songs. Like with other social media, new content keeps your audience engaged. Same thing here. Updated playlists with other artist's songs keeps the interest level in your songs high as well.

2. Do social shout-outs to any artist you add to your playlist. This is just good business, especially if it's an indie artist. They're more likely to return the favor, which is a good way to get exposure to a new audience.

3. Promote your playlists via newsletter and social. This is one that artists hardly ever consider. When you can't think of anything else to write or post about, promoting your playlist is always a good topic.

4. Re-assess the effectiveness of your playlist titles, descriptions, and artwork and make any necessary changes. Just like anything else you do online, these crucial details make a huge difference in engagement.

5. Encourage fans to follow you on Spotify. It seems simple, but its another detail frequently overlooked by artists.

6. Pin a new song or playlist to the top of your artist discography page. Pinning is a great strategy on any platform. Don't forget to use it.

7. Embed Spotify players on your website for all your albums. Links are not enough. Embed the player to be sure that you get that impulse play.

8. Check out your daily Spotify trending reports to better understand your audience and engagement on the platform to see what playlists include your music. You can't supply your audience with what it wants unless you know exactly what that is, and the trending reports can give you that information.

9. Give a social shout-out to any playlister who has added one of your songs. Just like on Facebook or Twitter, this can be very effective in maintaining the engagement of your fans.

10. Actually listen to your Discover Weekly playlist. This could be an easy way to find new tracks to add to your playlists. It's not always easy to find tracks that you like on your own, but the Discover Weekly playlist is there for reason. Use it.

These are a few small things that you can do to use the social aspects of Spotify to your benefit. They don't take much time, and can help increase both your audience and your streams.

13

Posting Frequency Strategy

You've read about post frequency throughout the book, but it's such an important concept that it deserves a chapter of its own. A musician using any kind of online promotion risks drawing the ire of his fans by posting too much, and lowering the marketing opportunities by posting too little. Obviously a balance must be struck, but posting frequency is not a one-size-fits-all situation; it must be tailored for each application.

Here's the game plan for posting not only on social media, but for content sites like your website and blog, as well as the latest strategy for releasing your videos and songs.

Posting On Social Media

While many have the opinion that you can never post too much on a social media network, research shows that there's definitely a threshold after which additional posts begin to feel like spam. That point varies for each network however. Let's look at the different points in all the major networks.

Facebook

Posting on a personal Facebook page has a different post limit than on a fan page. You've most certainly had friends that shortly after being introduced to Facebook felt that their every action during the day was of the utmost interest to everyone and as a result would post incessantly. Luckily, just at the point where you make the decision to block them they begin to realize that posting that much during a day is a lot of work and inherently back it off to a reasonable four or five times a day or less. Still others never quite get the message and end up being blocked by even their friends.

The limits on a fan or band page are far lower however, since fans expect only quality posts, and have a much lower post tolerance. Studies have found that the more you post, the less effective each post becomes. This is definitely a case of less is more. **Limit your posts to one per day; two at most.**

TIP: Play close attention to the number of unfollows or unlikes relative to your number of posts.

Twitter

Twitter is another case where a higher number of tweets on a personal account can be tolerated by your followers because the lifespan of each post is short (about an hour). There have been studies that have found that the average number of personal tweets range as high as 22 per day, and there are certainly circumstances where that many can be effective, like during a news-worthy event. Under most circumstances, more than four per hour lowers engagement considerably, and the possibility of a copy miscue that incites a flame war increases with each additional post.

As with Facebook, the frequency landscape for a brand account changes as well. Studies have found that the sweet spot is **between two and four per day**, with engagement dropping as the posts increase beyond that number. That said, some recent studies have found that 15 times a day can get good results.

Don't be afraid to thank anyone who either retweets a post or comments, although more than five to ten per day in your Twitter stream can also be deemed as excessive, in which case it's best to do a direct message instead.

TIP: Be sure to space out your posts throughout the day. Too many tweets at once can clog up your follower's Twitter streams or may even be considered spam by some.

Instagram

Instagram is pretty much of the opposite of most social networks in that the more you post, the more Likes and followers you get, according to a set of 14 studies looked at by CoSchedule.

That can be a little deceiving however, since it's been found that, like blogging, consistency in posting is what counts. The result of these studies is that you should **post on Instagram every day but only once (twice at most)** to get the most engagement and increase your followers.

LinkedIn

LInkedIn is very much like Instagram in that consistency really matters, but there are stricter limitations. For best results, **post only once every other day.**

Posting On Blogs

As stated in Chapter 11, blogging is all about the commitment to post in a timely fashion, but choosing that time can be somewhat daunting at first, especially if you've not blogged before. As someone who posts every weekday, I can tell you that doing it well does take time, so the amount of time that you have to spend on creating a post is a big part of the decision on your posting frequency.

That being said, if you want to build a reputation and an audience you should post at least once a day. A generally accepted amount for a "power blogger" is between three and five times per day. This is reserved more for the likes of a blog that's built as a news aggregator or source like MacDailyNews, Hypebot or TechCrunch, where the blog receives the blogger's full attention.

I believe that posting once a week is just barely enough to sustain an audience, but twice a week can be sufficient enough to grow it. As said before, more so than any other communication type online, blogs require a specific time and frequency to be successful. Once those have been determined, you must stick to that decision.

Updating Your Website

While it's true that research has shown that websites with a high update frequency generate more repeat visits per month, we all know just how difficult that update process can be, especially if your site is built traditionally off-line by a web designer and not as part of a blogging or DIY platform. While your site update frequency by itself doesn't directly effect your rankings, it does affect the user experience, and that's one of the major criteria that search engines rely on today when determining search ranking.

Google's spiders regularly crawl the web to rebuild its index, and the frequency that they crawl your site is a determining factor in how often your site needs to be updated. For instance, if you update your site every week but it's only crawled every month, then one of the reasons for updating it in the first place is negated. Of course, if you don't really care about your page rank and just want to concentrate on the user experience of the site, then a more frequent update makes sense. You can have both though, since there are many ways to improve Google spider crawling frequency, such as:

1. submitting a directory and sitemap to Google (Google allows you to submit a sitemap once per hour).

2. using social bookmarking sites.

3. adding fresh content to the website on a daily basis.

4. using a signature that has your site address on forums where you comment to get your website crawled.

5. modifying your meta tags regularly.

That said, a site should ideally be updated **once a quarter** if for no other reason than to add a new look or new content to attract returning visitors, although another criteria to use is any drop in traffic.

Newsletter Frequency

The frequency that you mail your newsletters is extremely important to the open rate, length of engagement, and click throughs. Send a newsletter too frequently and those measurements will fall, email not enough and you lose the advantage of the newsletter, which is for keeping your fans informed. Ultimately, the ideal frequency rate comes down to your business, your audience, and your content quality.

Even if you're a musician, the type of business that you run can vary widely. For instance, if your major priority is to inform your fans about your upcoming gigs, then once a week might seem about right. If the newsletter is more to keep in touch about major events like song and video releases, then once every four to eight weeks could be sufficient. If your merch business is strong and you have new items constantly coming available, then once a week could work. Some sales sites like eBay Deals, Woot and DealMac, or news sites, can mail every day without the list subscriber feeling intruded upon.

The tolerance of your audience for email is something that you'll have to gauge. Do you promise a certain frequency when they first subscribe? Do you see more than 5% unsubscribes with each mailing? These can indicate that either you're mailing too frequently or your content quality isn't high enough.

Content quality is probably the most important criteria. If you have news that your fans look forward to that doesn't feel like a constant bombardment of promotion, they can probably stand a frequency rate of once per week. If you're not sure what to include or are searching for material, then it's probably best to wait until there's no question that you have enough quality material.

All that said, for an artist or band, the sweet spot frequency for a newsletter mailing is **every four to six weeks**, which is just long enough from the last one that it's welcome, yet not long enough that you're forgotten. It's possible to push the time between posts to 12 weeks if you're in a dormant period and don't have much that's newsworthy, but any longer than that and you risk being ignored.

Posting Videos

Videos are different from the above networks in that a polished music video can't be produced quickly, but what's off-the-cuff and behind the scenes shot from your smartphone can. In fact, sometimes these impromptu videos are the ones that are the best received precisely because they're not slick and show your human side.

That said, when it comes to video, less is more. If you're doing just a quick smartphone movie, then **once every two to three days** is optimum, but more often can be possibly tolerated if you're shooting something that's newsworthy. If you're at a trade show, for instance, and keep running into celebrities that are willing to speak to you on camera, more frequent posts can be acceptable. Even in that case though, the best strategy is to save them for later and space their releases out, either over the course of a day, or even better, over a longer period of time.

Releasing Music

A new strategy in releasing music is beginning to take place, even within the major labels. In almost a return to the early days of records, the single song is king rather than the album, and that requires an entirely new look at the timing of when your material becomes available.

Back in the 1950s and '60s, the music world revolved around the single. Many artists we're signed for only a single or two that would have to be successful before the label would commit to making an album. If they finally got to that point, recording the entire album could be done in only a day or two since the number of tracks to recording on were limited. As technology evolved and recording track counts increased, overdubbing became possible so artists were able to not only perfect their performances, but also be a lot more creative as well, and this led to the creation of an album taking more and more time.

There was a lot more money in albums than there were singles, and as music sales took off, the record labels were more apt to spend more time making an album because of the potential profit involved. Slowly but surely, the two album per year norm of the '60s became one per year, then one every two years, then even longer. As far as the consumer was concerned, the wait for an album was hard enough, but what if there were only one or two good songs on it? Even a hit artist's fan base could actually dissipate if the product didn't come at regular intervals and feel like it was worth the wait.

Digital music turned that thinking upside down in that the fan could now cherry pick only the songs he wanted. As a result, music returned to the singles world that it is today, which brings about a new philosophy regarding recordings and how they are released, since albums are no longer the focus of the fan or audience.

Fewer Songs More Often

The basic premise of the new release philosophy is to release fewer songs but do it more frequently. In other words, it's better to release a song or two every six, eight, or twelve weeks than to wait a year for one album release of ten songs as was once done. Shorter release times benefit the artist in the following ways:

- The artist keeps their fans happy with a constant supply of new music. New music keeps the buzz and dialog going about the artist on the social networks.

- Each release is a separate marketing event. With the release of an album, you have one single event to publicize with a long period of time until the next one is produced. With individual releases, you have the potential for 11 separate releases (ten singles plus the album), which means that there's constantly new music in your fanbase ecosystem, and increased potential to reach new fans as a result.

- The artist gains increased exposure for every song. In a ten song album release, it's easy for a fan, reviewer or radio programmer to focus on just one or two of the songs while the others fall in priority. With individual releases, each song gets equal attention and has the ability to live and die on its own merits.

- An album can still be compiled after all the songs have been individually released. At the end of the year, or at the end of the artist's creative cycle, the songs are then put into an album that can be released in any format. The advantage is that the album has much advanced exposure and publicity thanks to previously released singles. Plus it can be treated as a marketing event to the artist's advantage.

Make no mistake, the album format is not dead in Music 4.0 (although sales continue to decrease), but the emphasis has shifted to the individual song. Not only that, the tastes and attention span of audiences today are shorter and shorter, which makes multiple releases an ideal fit with the lifestyle. No one is saying that you can't release an album; just that multiple singles at regular intervals before the album release work better in today's marketplace.

Remember that in our Music 4.0 world, your music is your marketing, not your product. Your social world is ultimately built around it, so the more frequently new music is available will benefit you greatly by providing more chances for fans hear it, and for potential fans to find it.

Glossary

above the fold: the upper half of the front page of a newspaper where a headline, important news story or photograph is often located. On a webpage, the text on the screen before you scroll down.

Adsense: a Google service for supplying advertisements to a website based on factors such as the website's content and the user's geographical location.

alt attribute: alternative text that's rendered when an element like a graphic on a web page can't be displayed. Also used by screen reader software so that a blind person listening to the page understands the element.

Arbitron ratings: a measurement of the number of people listening to a radio station at any given time period.

art: a creative endeavor that you do for your own personal satisfaction.

autoresponder: a program that automatically answers emails sent to it.

avatar: a graphical representation of the user's alter ego or character.

B2B: business to business.

B2C: business to consumer.

backlink: an outside link on another website that's connected to your page or blog.

banner: a form of Internet advertising.

barcode: a series of vertical bars of varying widths in which the numbers 0 through 9 are represented by a unique pattern of bars that can be read by a laser scanner. Barcodes are commonly found on consumer products and are used for inventory control purposes and, in the case of CDs, to tally sales for the purposes of chart position.

bashtag: the use of a person or company's Twitter hashtag to bash them or their products.

blip: a cross between a song and a tweet.

blog: a discussion or informational page on the Web consisting of discrete chronological posts.

Blogosphere: all blogs, their connections and communities.

bootleg: an unauthorized recording of a concert, a rehearsal, an outtake, or an alternate mix from an album.

brand: a name, sign, or symbol used to identify the items or services of a seller that differentiates them from their competitors. A brand is a promise of quality and consistency.

branding: the promotion of a brand.

brick and mortar: a physical retail store, which is usually composed of building materials like bricks and mortar.

catalog: older albums or recordings under the control of the record label. A release older than 18 months is considered catalog.

click-through: the number of times a link is clicked

co-branding: two firms working together to promote a product or service.

codec: a device or algorithm dedicated to encoding and decoding a digital stream. Usually used in audio and video.

collectible: an item (usually nonessential) that has particular value to its owner because of its rarity or desirability.

conglomerate: a multi-industry company or a large company that owns smaller companies in different businesses.

craft: a creative endeavor that you do for someone else's approval.

crowdfunding: a method of raising money for a project by offering incentives for fans to pool their money.

distribution network: The various retail sales outlets or, in the case of Music 4.0, digital music streaming sites.

DIY: do it yourself.

Edgerank: a news feed formula that Facebook has created to determine which stories are the most relevant to a user.

ESP: Email Service Providers.

flame war: hostile or insulting interaction between blog or forum commenters.

Flash: a program by Adobe used for creating short-form animation with a small enough file size that it can be used on the Web. Now obsolete.

frames: an outdated and graphically ugly method of displaying multiple HTML documents on a single webpage.

Google Alert: email updates of the latest relevant Google results (web, news, etc.) based on a set of chosen criteria.

Google Voice: a phone service offered by Google.

hashtags: the pound symbol (#) placed directly in front of a word in a tweet or Instagram post so it acts as a keyword.

heritage artist: a superstar act from the past that is still active. Madonna, Tina Turner, The Rolling Stones, and The Eagles are examples of current heritage acts.

image map: an easy way of adding hyperlinks to various parts of an image.

ISP: Internet Service Provider.

kbps: kilobits per second, or the amount of digital information sent per second. Sometimes referred to as "bandwidth."

keyword: a word or phrase that is closely linked to, or describes, a subject or website.

keyword stuffing: when a page is overloaded with keywords in an effort to be recognized by a search engine. Most search engines no longer respond to keywords as a result.

landing page: the home page or page that a user lands on after clicking on a link from a search engine.

Like: a button that allows Facebook users to show their support for a specific comment, status, picture wall post, or fan page.

Like-gating: an attempt to increase Likes more quickly than otherwise possible by providing exclusive content or prizes in exchange for Liking a page.

lurker: one who reads a blog but doesn't participate or post himself.

meet and greet: a brief meeting with an artist where the fans get to say hello, ask a few questions, and take pictures.

metadata: data about other data or content.

meta tags: html page data, which can typically include the Title, Description, and Keywords. For a song file, this might also include record label, songwriters, publisher and more.

micropayment: a means for transferring very small amounts of money in situations where collecting such small amounts of money is impractical or very expensive using the usual payment systems.

millennial: a member of the generation of children born between 1977 and 1994.

MP3: the contraction of MPEG-2 Audio Layer III, which at one time was the standard data-compression format used to make audio files smaller in size.

Music 4.0: the current generation of the music business, in which the artist can now communicate, interact with, market and sell directly to the fan. Record labels, radio, and television have become less relevant in Music 4.0, and many more single songs are consumed instead of albums.

opt-in: when someone provides permission to receive an email.

paid download: a downloadable song that you buy and own.

pay-per-click: an Internet advertising model used by search engines, advertising networks, and content sites such as blogs, in which advertisers pay their host only when their ad is clicked on.

paid search: a type of contextual advertising in which website owners pay an advertising fee to have their website shown in the top placement on search-engine results pages.

peer to peer: a type of transient Internet network that allows a group of computer users with the same networking program to connect with each other and directly access files from one another's hard drives.

P2P: see the entry under "peer to peer."

pirating: an illegal copy of a digital file, CD, CD artwork, or any other creative product, that is sold for a profit, but the record label, artist, and songwriter never takes part in the profit or provided royalties.

pop-ups: a form of advertising where unwanted and unexpected browser windows open automatically.

pull-down menu: also called a drop-down menu, where the item you select is at the top of the display, and the menu appears just below it when moused over, as if you had pulled it down.

QR Code: a graphic code similar to a bar code that provides a link to a website when scanned. An analog web link.

relevance: the manner in which keywords are related to the content of a page or search engine query.

record: a generic term for the distribution method of a recording. Regardless of whether it's vinyl, a CD, or a digital file, it's still known as a record.

RSS: Real Simple Syndication is a family of Web-feed formats used to publish frequently updated works such as blog entries, news headlines, audio, and video in a standardized format.

SERP: Search Engine Results Page.

sentiment: determining the attitude of a page visitor with regards to the content.

SEM: Search-Engine Marketing.

SEO: Search-Engine Optimization.

skin: a custom graphical interface.

smartphone: a mobile phone with advanced features such as Internet access, GPS tracking, and a camera.

spam: unsolicited advertising messages.

splash page: an introduction page of a website that sometimes features animation and appears prior to the home page.

superfan: a fan that is more passionate than the average fan.

swag: another name for merchandise, such as T-shirts, that is sold at a concert or on a website.

tag: a word or phrase that conveys the most important aspects of a product or website to help users search for content.

tag cloud: a graphical box containing a list of tags with the most prominent or popular tags receiving a darker and bigger font than less popular tags.

troll: someone who posts inflammatory off-topic messages with the intent of provoking a response.

tweet: a Twitter posting.

widget: a small application with limited and specific functioning.

watermarking: a recognizable image or pattern that's encoded into digitized music, video, or a graphic.

About Bobby Owsinski

Producer/engineer Bobby Owsinski is one of the best selling authors in the music industry with 23 books that are now staples in audio recording, music, and music business programs in colleges around the world, including the *The Mixing Engineer's Handbook*, *Deconstructed Hits series*, *Music 4.1 Internet Music Guidebook,* and more. He's also a contributor to Forbes writing on the new music business, his popular blogs have passed 7 million visits, and he's appeared on CNN and ABC News as a music branding and audio expert.

Visit Bobby's music production blog at bobbyowsinskiblog.com, his Music 3.0 music industry blog at music3point0.com, his Forbes blog at forbes.com/sites/bobbyowsinski/, his podcast at bobbyoinnercircle.com, and his website at bobbyowsinski.com.

Bobby Owsinski Bibliography

The Mixing Engineer's Handbook 4th Edition (BOMG Publishing)

The Recording Engineer's Handbook 4th Edition (BOMG Publishing)

The Mastering Engineer's Handbook 4th Edition (BOMG Publishing)

The Drum Recording Handbook 2nd Edition [with Dennis Moody] (Hal Leonard Publishing)

How To Make Your Band Sound Great (Hal Leonard Publishing)

The Studio Musician's Handbook [with Paul ILL] (Hal Leonard Publishing)

Music 4.1 - A Survival Guide To Making Music In The Internet Age 4th Edition (Hal Leonard Publishing)

The Music Producer's Handbook 2nd Edition (Hal Leonard Publishing)

The Musician's Video Handbook (Hal Leonard Publishing)

Mixing And Mastering With T-Racks: The Official Guide (Course Technology PTR)

The Touring Musician's Handbook (ISBN 978-1423492368 Hal Leonard)

The Ultimate Guitar Tone Handbook [with Rich Tozzoli] (Alfred Music Publishing)

The Studio Builder's Handbook [with Dennis Moody] (Alfred Music Publishing)

Abbey Road To Ziggy Stardust [with Ken Scott] (Alfred Music Publishing)

The Audio Mixing Bootcamp (Alfred Music Publishing)

Audio Recording Basic Training (Alfred Music Publishing)

The Music 3.0 Guide To Social Media. *Tips and Tricks for using Facebook, Twitter, YouTube and Google+.* (BOMG Publishing)

Social Media Promotion For Musicians *The Manual For Marketing Yourself, Your Band or your Music Online* (BOMG Publishing)

Social Media Promotion For Small Business and Entrepreneurs *The Manual for Marketing Yourself or your Business Online* (BOMG Publishing)

Deconstructed Hits: Classic Rock Vol. 1 (Alfred Music Publishing)

Deconstructed Hits: Modern Pop & Hip-Hop (Alfred Music Publishing)

Deconstructed Hits: Modern Rock & Country (Alfred Music Publishing)

The PreSonus StudioLive Mixer Official Manual (Alfred Music Publishing)

You can get more info and read excerpts from each book by visiting the excerpts section of bobbyowsinski.com.

Courses Available From Bobby Owsinski

Vocal Mixing Techniques

The Music Mixing Primer

101 Mixing Tricks

Hit Makers Club

All of the above courses and more are part of Bobby's Hit Makers Club membership. Find out more at hitmakersclub.com

Bobby Owsinski Lynda.com Video Courses

The Audio Mixing Bootcamp Video Course

Audio Recording Techniques

Mastering For iTunes

Audio Mastering Techniques

Music Studio Setup and Acoustics

Selling Music Merchandise

Selling Your Music: CDs, Streams and Downloads

Bookmarking Sites for Musicians and Bands

Pinterest for Musicians and Bands

Google+ for Musicians and Bands

YouTube for Musicians and Bands

Blogging Strategies for Musicians and Bands

Twitter for Musicians and Bands

Mailing List Management for Musicians and Bands

Website Management for Musicians and Bands

Facebook for Musicians and Bands

Social Media Basics for Musicians and Bands

Find out more at Lynda.com

Bobby Owsinski's Online Connections

Music Production Blog: bobbyowsinskiblog.com

Music Industry Blog: music3point0.com

Forbes Blog: forbes.com/sites/bobbyowsinski/

Facebook: facebook.com/bobby.owsinski

YouTube: youtube.com/polymedia

Pinterest: pinterest.com/bobbyowsinski/

Linkedin: linkedin.com/in/bobbyo

Twitter: @bobbyowsinski

Website: bobbyowsinski.com

Courses: bobbyowsinskicourses.com

An Instructor Resource Kit for this book is available.

Everything you need to begin using *Social Media Promotion For Musicians* in your course right now!

Each kit includes:

- Syllabus

- Topics for Demonstrations and Discussions for each chapter

- Test Bank and answer key for 12 week semester

- Powerpoint and Keynote presentations for each chapter

The *Social Media Promotion For Musicians* Instructor Resource Kit <u>is free</u>.

Send an email to office@bobbyowsinski.com to receive the download link.